BATTLE PLAN

Confronting Strongholds Men Face Today

Real talk with
Ernie Stuckey

WESTBOW
PRESS®
A DIVISION OF THOMAS NELSON
& ZONDERVAN

WestBow Press books may be ordered through booksellers or by contacting:

WestBow Press
A Division of Thomas Nelson & Zondervan
1663 Liberty Drive
Bloomington, IN 47403
www.westbowpress.com
1 (866) 928-1240

ISBN: 978-1-9736-5093-5 (sc)
ISBN: 978-1-9736-5092-8 (hc)
ISBN: 978-1-9736-5094-2 (e)

Library of Congress Control Number: 2019900334

Print information available on the last page.

WestBow Press rev. date: 11/11/2019

CONTENTS

INTRODUCTION

One late summer afternoon my fifteen-year-old daughter and I decided to drive into town to pick up dinner for the family. As we were traveling down the ocean side highway catching views of the Atlantic Ocean she began to cry. The next words that came out of her mouth were the words that are forever etched in my mind. "Dad, I want you to know you broke my heart a few years ago. I can't get over it and I've been mad at you ever since."

She went on to explain about a certain evening when the house phone rang around 3:00 a.m. Unbeknownst to me she answered the phone as I picked up the second line at the exact same time. She listened in on a conversation between my adulteress lover and me. The next morning my daughter confronted me in front of her mother. Not only did I deny the conversation, but I called my young daughter, who until then viewed me as her knight in shining armor, a liar.

Little did I know the ramifications and the lingering effects my sin would cause to my daughter. I had no idea that those words had crushed her and that all of this time she had kept this pain in her heart. I had confessed my affair to my family well over a year before this oceanside drive conversation with my daughter. I thought our little family was well on the road to recovery.

It was during this time I realized that simple little verse *"Thou shalt not commit adultery"* Exodus 20:14 (KJV), is only a headline to an action that cuts much deeper. In this one phrase, God gets directly to the point. He knows the pain we endure from this and all sins, and more importantly, the repercussions felt by a family when we commit such a self-indulgent act. I have come to realize that not only do we bring life changing sorrow to our wives, we also affect our children and friends. Entire families are disrupted, including "the other woman's" children, husband and friends.

It was that drive on a late summer afternoon which caused me to begin a lengthy analysis of my life. Not only did I have to examine my past and present, but I had to prepare for my future. Fast forward to today, twenty-three years later, I find myself ministering to hundreds of men who deal with an assortment of struggles and pain. Men who are looking for answers.

This book you hold in your hands may very well contain some answers. It may give you some insight on how to help others around you. I am not a professional writer, and I don't have a seminary degree. I am simply a man who has seen life at its worst and has experienced the healing power of our Creator.

My story is one of many I have encountered. God has blessed me to be able to walk beside other men during their darkest hours. In these pages are hard discussions and eye-opening truths. My hope is that you will be able walk with me through my journey so that you might work towards becoming better husbands, better fathers and better men. I have often heard people say that no one has ever written a book on how to be a man.

I disagree.

Today we live in a society where truth has become nothing more than the level of our comfort. We go through life living in the gray, where there is no more simplicity of black and white. We live in a modern-day Rome, where if it feels good, it's okay. Accountability is becoming a thing of the past, and we are comparing what is real to an unattainable fantasy of reality. We will just never measure up.

Regardless of how many toys or how much money we make, we still can't seem find that fulfillment or fill that void in the pit of our soul. We keep chasing dreams to one dead end after another. When will we acknowledge we simply don't know where to find that peace which constantly evades us?

I have found in life the simplest of pleasures are sometimes hidden in plain sight. For many of us this requires nothing more than to simply wipe the dust off a book we've tucked away in a closet. For forty-nine years of my life, I never realized something as simple as a book could contain such wisdom, knowledge and love until I took time to take in the words rather than rush through them as if I was preparing for a final exam.

Like many I assumed words in an ancient book could not possibly teach me how to live in the twenty-first century. Little did I know, the words contained in this book have been woven into the very fabric of our being. This book is called *The Holy Bible*. This is the book of life. It is the living, breathing word of God. When we read from a perspective of seeking rather than persecuting, the words jump from the pages and into our hearts. The more we read and learn, we begin to fill that void in our lives that God allowed in the first place for the very purpose of drawing us back to Him.

Let's look at it another way. Every man I know has a toolbox. Regardless of whether there are a few tools in his tool box or many, nothing speaks to a man's worth than having tools in which he can fix things. What we do not understand is every man also has a *spiritual toolbox*. My prayer is this book will be the key in which to help you unlock your spiritual toolbox, otherwise known as *The Holy Bible*. Contained inside of your spiritual toolbox are the tools that will help you repair whatever is broken in your life.

Often, we see the problem, but we do not know which is the proper tool to use. How many times have we found ourselves attempting to turn a screw with a Flat head screw driver when a Phillips head screwdriver is required? Some of you, like me, have a toolbox with limited tools. Having the proper life tools will help you gain the abundant life Jesus speaks of in the book of John, "*The thief comes only to steal and kill and destroy. I came that they may have life and have it abundantly*" John 10:10 (ESV).

Making the most of your tools requires having good instructions. To help men become a better father, husband and man we need more than just instructions. We need a *Battle Plan*. Within these pages is a time-tested battle plan which will help you to become the man God is calling you to be. I will share with you what I believe are the Top Ten Strongholds that are keeping men from living the abundant life spoken of by Jesus. We will take each stronghold and break it down to its core. Each chapter a *Strategic Attack Plan* using the tools God has already given us to gain victory. Did you know God has already equipped you for victory? Are you ready to open your spiritual toolbox? Let's get to work!

Sea Oats by Donna M. Courson

DEDICATION

I dedicate this book, first and foremost, to my wife Robyn who lived through the tough years with me, yet never left my side. To my daughters, Heather and Amber, for allowing me to demonstrate that it's never too late to change.

To my Pastors and Mentors - Ben Hall, Van Power, John Culbreth, Chip King, Lamar Underwood, Darryl Bellar, Jackie Hayes, Ben Guest, Dwayne Sumner, Mike Darby, Uncle Frank Stuckey, Jake Mottayaw, Sean Gossett, Bill Kearney, Uncle Duane Moyer, Bill Sullenger, Uncle Norman Stuckey, Steve Farford, Tom Moore and David Drake. You are my Paul.

To Coaches – Dave Husky, Derek Hulsey, Jerry Rice, Jonathan Williams.

To Gary Gaskill, Bob Boyne, Paul James, Nick Gaskill, Adam Salzburg, Charles Deringer, Chris Spivey, Chuck Lynch, Dan Morris, David McIntire, Derek Mallett, Derek Bellar, Glenn Parrish, Greg Beavers, Dan Binette, Herman Cook, Jerry Knowles, Jimmie Fender, Lance Jones, Mike Rineck, Ben Buben, Nick Deonas, Razor Ray Matz, Roy Kunkle, Kalvin Thompson and Scott Schol. You are my Barnabas.

To the many men whom I have had the privilege to minister to over the years. You are my Timothy.

To the men who believed in the mission of the Christian Men's Association of North Florida, the Family Driven Softball League and Encourage Ministries.

To my Dad, Lamar Stuckey. Even after your death you have never stopped teaching me.

To Jason Pust. You have left a hole in my heart. I think of you everyday.

To Kevin Carden and Donna M. Courson for contributing photos.
To Dan Binette and Heather Mallett for content editing.

And more important than any name mentioned. To my Lord and Savior Jesus Christ. Words can never explain the love I have for You. You have taught me to love others despite who they are, because You love me in spite of who I am.

Proceeds from this book will be donated to Huntington's Disease Research. For more information go to www.hdsa.org

CHAPTER ONE

Strongholds

W hat are strongholds? Merriam-Websters describes a stronghold as, "An area where most people have the same beliefs, values etc.: an area dominated by a certain group:

a protected place where the members of a military group stay and can defend themselves against attacks."

But what if this certain group built for themselves a stronghold intended for evil?

Since the beginning of mankind there has been good and evil. Most people believe there is some sort of ongoing war between the two. More often than not, we believe evil wins. The fact of the matter is the only reason evil exists at all is because God allows it to exist. The proof of this statement regarding the battle between good and evil can be found in the book of Job when Satan had to ask God permission to tempt Job. "*The Lord said to Satan, 'Very well, then, everything he has is in your power, but on the man, himself do not lay a finger.' Then Satan went out from the presence of the Lord*". Job 1:12 (NIV). Satan and all his demons have never been, nor will they ever be, a match for God.

There are many verses in the Bible that proves this fact, but the scripture that stands out to me the most can be found in a story in the book of Matthew.

> "*And when He came to the other side, to the country of the Gadarenes, two demon-possessed men met Him, coming out of the tombs, so fierce that no one could pass that way. And behold, they cried out, "What have you to*

do with us, O Son of God? Have you come to torment us before the time?" Now a herd of many pigs was feeding at some distance from them. And the demons begged Him, saying, "If you cast us out, send us away into the herd of pigs." And He said "Go." So, they came out and went into the pigs, and behold, the whole herd rushed down the steep bank into the sea and drowned in the waters." Matthew 8:28-32 ESV.

Several things happen in this scripture that is worth noting: (1) The demons recognized Jesus. (2) They were very afraid of Him. (3) Knowing that a fight would be futile, they never attempted to raise a hand to Jesus. (4) They had to ask permission to go to the pigs.

Yet knowing the power of God, we still give in to the evil that exists today. I believe the hardest thing God has ever done was stand by as His son hung, bled and died on the cross. I believe the second hardest thing God did was to give us, His beloved creation, the choice to deny Him.

Of course, we understand why. What joy would there be if God created us like robots? We would all look the same, behave the same and think the same. The action of love would all be the same because we would have no choice. As fathers even if we could force our children to love us, it clearly would not be the same.

Spiritual strongholds

Like all sin, spiritual strongholds are a battle of the mind that can affect our physical well being. Transformation strategist Ed Salvoso defines a spiritual stronghold as "a mindset impregnated with hopelessness that causes us to accept something that we know is contrary to the will of God." The apostle Paul defines strongholds as a mindset raised up against the knowledge of God. It is any type of thinking that exalts itself above God, therefore allowing Satan to influence an individual's mind. This is the very reason why conquering our strongholds may very well be the most important battle we will face in our lives.

God has given us knowledge through His word on how to conquer strongholds. This gift is available to everyone. However we must learn how to use that gift which is our spiritual tool box. I am not a professional counselor with a college degree hanging on my wall, but what I am is a sinner saved by grace and a man who has a passion for helping men become better fathers, husbands and men of accountability. My training in this field comes from wallowing in the sewage of my own sin and being pulled from the pits of hell from a God who listened to my wife who prayed for me without ceasing.

God took my mess and turned it into a message. I know beyond a shadow of a doubt God desires this for every man regardless of his age, color or disposition. I will not only answer questions regarding strongholds we men face today, but offer a battle plan on how to defeat these strongholds.

Why is there sin?

We know living in God's will is best for us, but we allow the pleasure of sin to control our being. Why would God allow sin in the first place? Because we were given free will! Our free will means we can choose to go against God's perfect will. Sin is anything that separates us from God. God had to establish boundaries in order to protect us from ourselves. Did you know there is one thing God cannot do? God cannot participate in sin. Therefore, God cannot have a relationship with us if we are living in sin. It's like a human being trying to breath water. One of the most powerful events in history is found in Matthew 27:46 when God turns His face from Jesus. At that moment our Savior took on the sin of the world. God His own father cannot look upon His only son because He cannot look upon sin. What makes us think we are any different? Yet God still desires a personal relationship with us with the promise of a future *"For I know the thoughts that I think toward you, says the Lord, thoughts of peace and not of evil, to give you a future and a hope"*. (Jeremiah 29:11 NKJV).

Our sin nature

We also have a "sin nature". The term "original sin" as revealed in the Book of Genesis in chapter three is the story of when Adam and Eve defied God by eating from the Tree of Knowledge of Good and Evil.

This act resulted in the rest of mankind inheriting a propensity to sin, commonly referred to as having a "sin nature". Sin nature is the aspect in man that makes us rebellious against God. We have a natural inclination to sin when given the choice to do God's will or our own. We will naturally choose to follow our own desires.

God knows our struggles and understands our battles. He also understands the temptation of sin. I have often heard people say that God will never give you something you can't handle. I do not agree. God will absolutely place obstacles and tragedies in your life in order to draw you closer to Him. *"If you endure chastening, God deals with you as with sons; for what son is there whom a father does not chasten?"* Hebrews 12:7 NKJV. Sometimes we will face challenges, or even tragedy, not as punishment but as an opportunity to grow your own faith. When this happens remember:

> *"No temptation has overtaken you except such as common to man; but God is faithful, who will not allow you to be tempted beyond what you are able, but with the temptation will also make a way of escape, that you may be able to bear it."* 1 Corinthians 10:13 NKJV.

"But God demonstrates His own love toward us, in that while we were still sinners, Christ died for us." Romans 5:8. (NKJV). Never forget the reason why Jesus came to Earth in the first place, to die for our sins because God loves us that much. Jesus took our place at Calvary, so we could have an opportunity to live a life with God. Not just in Heaven, but right here where you live.

> *"For God so loved the world He gave His only begotten Son, that whoever believes in Him should not perish but have everlasting life. For God did not send His Son into the world to condemn the world, but that the world through Him might be saved."* John 3:16-17 NKJV

When we cry out to God, He hears our every prayer. Sometimes when God does not answer our prayers, it does not mean He is not listening. Sometimes it may mean He is showing us that we are not ready. When God is walking beside you through a crisis, you can rest assured God's promise in 1 Corinthians 10:13 is true! God will absolutely chasten those He loves in order to draw, punish or teach them

Ten major strongholds

In my personal experience and years of discipling men, I have noticed ten major strongholds. Before we attack the stronghold, we must identify the stronghold. Here are the ten major strongholds I have found:

- Addictions
- Anger
- Depression
- Discipline
- Fear
- Jealousy
- Leading your family
- Lust
- Pride
- Unforgiveness

In the pages that follow, I will present a Battle Plan on how to confront and defeat these strongholds. In chapter two we will learn the power of making real resolutions. In chapters three through twelve we will take each stronghold and break it down to its very core. Once we gain victory, our final chapter will teach us how to maintain success.

Level of severity

There are three levels of strongholds to be considered in regards to the battle of the mind. Often, we never consider our way of thinking can destroy our body as well. Like someone who suffers from diabetes, if left uncontrolled, they end up destroying their body.

Those who struggle with strongholds are unaware of the effect on our everyday lives and the damage it causes within.

We must first determine the level of severity. When we deal with emotions like jealousy, anger, and fear we must ask ourselves if they are nothing more than passing thoughts or bad habits. Do they consume our everyday lives? Often times a stronghold such as anger can also fuel other bad habits such as jealousy, pride, and addictions. We find when an emotion such as anger is controlled, we benefit by having less stress concerning these other unhealthy emotions. There are times when we know which stronghold is damaging our lives and the lives of our loved ones. We know the benefit of purging the stronghold but laziness, lack of discipline or spiritual warfare gets in the way.

Often a spiritual stronghold will reveal itself to those we love much sooner than we realize the grip that it has on us. We promise to change and for a while, things get better. Unfortunately before too long, this addiction raises its ugly head once more, bringing more heartache with the added bonus of letting our loved ones down. Since we did not have a strategic plan on how to confront and defeat the stronghold, we often fall back into the darkness causing our loved ones to deal with our shortcomings again and again.

Prescribed medications

There are certain professionally prescribed medicines available today that can help with some of these strongholds, but medication can only take you so far. So, should we continue to take these medications? Absolutely. God created medicine to help us. However until we seek help from the great physician, that is God, we will never receive a complete healing. To defeat any stronghold, we must view it for what it really is, a sickness. And we must be willing to do whatever is necessary to get well. We must also recognize the sickness for what it truly is: a battle *within* the mind. Until we confront this sin, darkness will creep upon us.

I have learned most men don't know where to start when attacking their strongholds. Sometimes it's easy to identify the issue, but until we learn its origin and what feeds it, we cannot strategically mount a plan to defeat it. Every man needs a battle plan. This is the purpose of this book, to help you build a strategic battle plan to confront the sin and gain victory.

Our Battle Plan

Within our Battle plan there are three components needed to obtain success.

1) Confront the sin
2) Seek forgiveness
3) Answer the call

Together we will address these three components and help you identify which stronghold is keeping you from living the abundant life God has promised you. We will then help you discover the necessary tools within your spiritual toolbox to help you defeat your stronghold. Finally, at the end of each chapter you will find a question and answer page designed to help you in your journey of maintaining victory. We will find our answers through the word of God.

> *"For the weapons of our warfare are not carnal but mighty in God for pulling down strongholds, casting down arguments and every high thing that exalts itself against the knowledge of God, bringing every thought into captivity to the obedience of Christ, and being ready to punish all disobedience when your obedience is fulfilled."* 2 Corinthians 10:4-6 NKJV

DISCUSSION

1) Where does a stronghold come from? _____

2) What are your thoughts on the statement "God will never give you something you can't handle"? _____

3) Regarding the severity of your stronghold. Do you believe your stronghold is a Passing thought?

   _____

   A bad habit?

   _____

   It consumes your everyday life?

   _____

4) How do you feel about taking prescription medication for strongholds such as addictions, anger, depression etc.?

   _____

   _____

   _____

   _____

5) Do you believe God can heal every sickness?
   Yes ____ No ____
   Why?_____

   _____

   _____

6) Do you have a spiritual tool box?
   _____Yes _____No

7) Read 2 Corinthians 10: 4-6. What are your thoughts on this passage? _____

   _____

   _____

   _____

Chapter Two (Resolutions), will help you to identify strongholds and its effects.

CHAPTER TWO

Resolutions

In Bob Barnes book *Men Under Construction* he said, "A good man is a gift to all who know him – he's dependable like the sunrise because his goodness springs from inner strength, and not outward circumstance." How many times have we allowed our outward circumstance to determine who we are? Where does our inner strength come from? When difficulty or tragedy invades our lives, do we think maybe it is a consequence of our sin? Are we under attack because Satan knows God has a plan for our lives?

Perhaps God allows things to happen because it will help us to become better men. We all have issues in our lives that we deal with daily. But do we believe God can take our mess and turn it into a message?

> "We can rejoice, too, when we run into problems and trials, for we know that they help us develop endurance. And endurance develops strength of character, and character strengthens our hope of salvation." Romans 5:3-4 (NLT). "Because you know that the testing of your faith produces perseverance." James 1:3 NIV.

Making a Resolution

We often compare the idea of making a resolution with the beginning of a new year. Forbes.com reports that 40% of Americans make New Year's resolutions, but by February, 80% have failed. Research indicates only 8% of those who make new year's resolutions actually succeed.

Why do people fail so miserably at making resolutions? Because like in many situations today, we are no longer held accountable for our actions. We spend a vast amount of time focusing on things that have little or no significance in our lives. Patrick Morely from the book *Man in the Mirror* said, "Perhaps the greatest weakness we men face today is that we tend to lead unexamined lives." Family time has been replaced by fast food, sports arenas and a misguided American dream.

Definition of Resolution

A New Year's Resolution, according to Wikipedia, is when *a person resolves to change an undesired trait or behavior in order to accomplish a personal goal or otherwise change their life.*

My father resolved to quit smoking every year, but never succeeded. In 1993, he died of lung cancer leaving behind a wife, two sons and eight grandchildren. My brother resolved to stop abusing drugs and alcohol every year, but never succeeded. In 1998, his body simply shut down from years of physical neglect. He died leaving behind five children.

In 2015, I received a message from a man claiming to be my son. Being very skeptical, I prayed about it. In the fall of 2017, I resolved to finally meet this man. We agreed that I would travel to Mobile, Alabama, meet with him, have lunch and a DNA test completed. I was set to determine, once and for all, whether I had a son that I never knew.

On September 26th I received a message that my son was found dead in his home with no answer as to why. I made that planned trip to Mobile, to preach at his funeral and to have follow through with the DNA test. A week later while sitting in the Charlotte Airport, I learned with complete certainty that I had a son. My son's name was Jason. For no apparent reason. he died at the age of 42. His sister and his best friend told me that Jason dreamed of the day he would finally get to meet his Dad, me. I never was able to touch him or look into his eyes to tell him how sorry I was for not being there for his life and for not fully believing him when he found me.

God is a God of Second Chances

My father made a resolution to stop smoking. My brother made a resolution to get off drugs and take better care of himself. I made a resolution to put a very serious question to bed. None of us accomplished our resolutions. Despite of our sin, it's never too late! Many of us marvel at the omnipotence of God, but in truth the greatest marvel about God is His power and willingness to forgive.

Is our sin greater than God's grace? Is accepting Jesus into our hearts enough or is it nothing more than punching our spiritual "get out of hell free" card? Is the reason God saved us in the first place is because He has a plan for our lives? He has a purpose for us.

How many times do we make a New Year's resolution and fail? Perhaps we fail because we believe that our failures are only affecting ourselves. This idea allows us to put our resolutions off to another day, month, or year. My father, my brother and I felt that way. We felt that we had all of the time in the world, until we didn't. What if we realized our very well-being is solely dependent on life change? What if we knew our spouses, our children and our friends would suffer because of our lackadaisical attitude regarding our resolution? What if we treated it like it was a matter of life or death?

Spiritual strongholds can result in death

We need to resolve to attack spiritual strongholds. They threaten the death of our relationships, marriages, respect and love from our children. They can also threaten the death of our physical body, positivity and, most of all, the death of a relationship with our Father, God.

We cannot afford to wait until a new year. We must confront our strongholds right here and right now. Our loved ones are counting on us. When making a resolution to confront and defeat these strongholds, we will need the support of others to counsel and hold us accountable. However we cannot ask this of our wives and children. We must seek assistance from someone for whom we trust to guide us through our journey.

Your Wife as an Accountability Partner

Our spouses are very good at holding us accountable from a preventative standpoint, but to ask our wives to hold us accountable in the beginning of a battle often leads to unfair pressure on them. They are left the burden of, not only working through the forgiveness stage for themselves, but also trying to keep us focused on winning our battle. This ends up pulling the spouse in two different directions, especially when they will be the most affected if or when we relapse or fail. We should not ask our wives to take on this burden. This does not mean we should keep the knowledge of our struggles secret from our spouses, just that we should not ask them to take on the responsibility of keeping us accountable in the early stages of our struggle.

Sometimes wives can serve as a successful accountability partner during an attack on a stronghold, but they must have a lot of support. When I admitted to my affair to my wife, we were both not walking with the Lord. If not for her knowledge of Christ as a child and understanding the power of prayer, she would have had no foundation through which to work. Yet even then, the struggles she went through nearly destroyed her. She was not prepared for the strife that she would face. I believe that had she been a deep-rooted Christian and was aware of her own spiritual toolbox, as she has now, her struggles would have been faced with more wisdom and discernment.

Nonetheless, I still strongly recommend only using the spouse as an accountability partner from a preventative measure and not as in an advisory capacity. A "preventative position" means that once you have shared your struggles and committed to making a change, your spouse could offer you encouragement and reminders of your goal. As in the case of sexual addictions, her role could be to monitor what you view on the computer, movies, television, etc. You should always share with her what you are thinking and how you are feeling. It helps her to understand your experience.

The *advisory* part of accountability should always come from someone who possess a greater knowledge of God's word than the both of you and someone who is unafraid to confront you during moments of weakness.

Using your children as an accountability partner

I once had a man tell me he was using his fifteen-year-old son as his accountability partner. When I asked why, he said because "My son had a knack for understanding life." What life? This, to me, was an indicator of the father's lack of wisdom more than the son's wisdom.

When I teach small groups, often subject matter has a lot to do with who is in the class. One of my favorite curricula to teach is *33 The Series* from Authentic_Manhood. During the open discussion period, I separate the teens from the men simply because their level of processing and understanding are on two different spectrums. Men will naturally keep to themselves and not open up regarding their struggles around teens. By nature, they know a teen's experience in life is seen with limited wisdom. Regardless of what a teen is exposed to in life, there is no replacement for wisdom that comes with age and exposure. Knowledge is learned but wisdom is a gift from God.

We need other men, Godly men, who are unafraid of our wrath and who will counsel and hold us accountable. There is no better place than the local church for finding such men.

The Local Church and the Surgical Mask

If you are not a member of a Christian church, I strongly recommend finding one. When sharing the gospel, I encounter people who say "I want to go to church, but I need to get my life straight before going there." A church that gives the impression we must clean up our act before going to church, is not a good church. It is one that we should avoid attending. Just like a hospital, a real church is a place to go to get well.

In the winter of 2018 we had a flu epidemic in my hometown. Everywhere you went, department stores, movie theaters and even the local hospitals, many people were wearing surgical masks to protect them from the illnesses that everyone else was carrying. Regardless, they still went out in public and still functioned at life so that they could tend to their everyday duties. In order to protect themselves, some wore surgical masks Others wore surgical masks because they didn't want to give their sickness to others.

The difference with a real church is that we can assume all of us walking in the building has some sort of illness. We don't need to wear a surgical mask to claim that we are either well or sick. A church is a hospital for those of us who want to be well spiritually. Understand every church has someone who thinks they are above sin. Every church has someone who passes judgment on others. This is not right, and they do nothing to advance the Kingdom, but rather destroy the real purpose of church.

If this keeps you from going to church then perhaps you should quit your job, stop shopping or going to the movies. Everywhere you go, these types of people go also. Every church has a few people you really don't care to be around, just like in our community. Most churches also have people who are there to worship God and love on those of us who have crud (sin), in our lives. They understand everyone lives with sin even when a person claims perfection. If you do not attend a local church, then I suggest you go and seek out these people who are there for God's purpose and get well. When you walk in the doors of a real church, you will know because the real Christians will seek you out, rather than snub their nose at you.

Some may say they do not need to attend church in order to have a better relationship with God. They may say something like, "Well I can worship God anywhere. I don't need to go to church to worship God." That is another lie from hell.

"And let us consider one another in order to stir up love and good works, not forsaking the assembling of ourselves together, as is the manner of some, but exhorting one another, and so much more as you see the Day approaching." Hebrews 10:24-25 (NKJV).

This scripture states, "as is the manner of some," which is referring to those who do not believe they need church! This scripture also proclaims, "you see the Day is approaching." This is speaking of the day Christ returns to Earth. Christ will come again, and he will not be politically correct. Statistics show ten out of every ten people will die. Regardless of what a non-believer thinks, we are going to spend eternity somewhere. The "Day" as noted in Hebrews 10:25 is fast approaching and will happen.

If you do not have a Christian man in your life who is well versed in the word of God, find a church home and speak to the pastor about having an accountability partner. He will know what to do. I promise you nothing you can tell him will surprise him. Ask him about the churches men's ministry. Churches who have a vibrant men's ministry usually know how to deal with real issues we men face today.

Confronting the Stronghold

There is no time better than the present to confront the strongholds in our lives and begin living a productive life of happiness, hope and joy. We must resolve these issues, confront and destroy the strongholds that are keeping us from living the abundant life God has promised us.

Let's address some resolutions we can make that will impact those we love. When you read different studies and hear many professional opinions on this subject, they all differ as to which may be considered the most severe stronghold. Of the strongholds mentioned, virtually all of them rank in the top ten as well as are strongholds I have encountered when ministering to other men.

Let's address the Top Ten Strongholds I have found that are destroying our families today. As we begin, I want you to consider the scripture found in the book of John 10:10 (NKJV), "*A thief does not come except to steal, and to kill, and to destroy. I have come that they may have life, and that they may have it more abundantly.*"

Here are the Top Ten Strongholds we men face today:

- Addiction
- Anger
- Depression
- Discipline
- Fear
- Jealousy
- Leading your family
- UnForgiveness
- Lust
- Pride

I have formulated a scale to which I believe can help you identify and defeat your strongholds. As mentioned in Chapter One, when confronting our strongholds, we must first determine the severity of each one. When dealing with these issues is it merely a passing thought? A bad habit? Or is it consuming your everyday life?

A Passing Thought

The phrase "passing thought" can also be thought of as an impulse or notion. When we have passing thoughts regarding the Top Ten Strongholds, these are nothing more than a byproduct of our sin nature. Remember, because of our sin nature, things that are not of God will enter our minds. It's what we do with these thoughts whether it becomes sin.

> "You have heard that it was said to those of old, 'You shall not commit adultery.' But I say to you that whoever looks at a woman to lust for her has already committed adultery with her in his heart." Matthew 5:27-28 (NKJV).

Bad Habits

Wikipedia states "A bad habit is a negative behavior pattern. Common examples include: procrastination, overspending, nail biting or spending too much time watching television or using the computer." A key factor in distinguishing a bad habit from a stronghold is the element of will power. Wikipedia goes on to explain "If a person still seems to have control over the behavior, then it is just a bad habit. Good intentions are able to override the negative effect of bad habits, but their effect seems to be independent and additive – the bad habits remain but are subdued rather than canceled."

Three Strongholds that can Never be Considered just Bad Habits

Addictions, unforgiveness and lust can never rank in the bad habit category. These are strongholds regardless of what level we may consider them to be due to the emotional and physical damage these strongholds cause. A bad habit can be overridden with good intentions.

Having good intentions can never overcome addictions, unforgiveness or lust.

Consuming your Everyday Life

An article by Christian Armor Ministries states "A stronghold is an area of darkness within our mind or personality that causes ongoing spiritual, emotional and/or behavioral problems. We can genuinely be born-again, and sincere in our faith, but have ongoing struggles and thoughts, emotions, and habits that wage war against our relationship with Christ." A stronghold doesn't let go of our emotions. We deal with it daily. Sometimes we entertain these thoughts so frequently, we forget they are not normal. There are those who are so obsessed with anger, jealousy, pride etc. They exclude the fact that this is contrary to a healthy lifestyle. We lack the discipline or willpower to purge ourselves from the very act that is destroying our relationship with others and with God. So how do we determine whether these issues are simply passing thoughts, bad habits or strongholds?

Determining your Stronghold

In order to identify your stronghold and form a battle plan in defeating it, we must first answer these questions truthfully and ask a trusted friend these questions about ourselves. Do not ask someone to answer these questions who tends to agree with your every thought. We all know "yes men." I've had men come to me proclaiming to have no strongholds because a subordinate agreed with their findings. We sometimes don't see our shortcomings.

This is why it is good to ask your wife or another man of accountability who has known you for some time to participate in this test with you. Remember, no matter what they indicate on the test, you are not permitted to show anger towards them. Remember this is about making you well, not calling you out.

On a scale of one, being the most severe, and ten, being the least concern, respond by circling a number on every emotion or fault listed on this scale. You must only circle one number per emotion or fault.

Addictions	1	2	3	4	5	6	7	8	9	10
Anger	1	2	3	4	5	6	7	8	9	10
Depression	1	2	3	4	5	6	7	8	9	10
Discipline	1	2	3	4	5	6	7	8	9	10
Fear	1	2	3	4	5	6	7	8	9	10
Jealousy	1	2	3	4	5	6	7	8	9	10
Leading your family	1	2	3	4	5	6	7	8	9	10
Unforgiveness	1	2	3	4	5	6	7	8	9	10
Lust	1	2	3	4	5	6	7	8	9	10
Pride	1	2	3	4	5	6	7	8	9	10

If you circled any of these emotions or faults with the number seven through ten, chances are these issues are merely a passing thought. You will need to keep an eye on these issues, but clearly there is a bigger need. If you circled any of the emotions or faults numbers four through six, excluding addictions, unforgiveness or lust, these are bad habits and need to be addressed. (Remember, at no time can addictions, unforgiveness or lust be considered bad habits.) On any of the emotions or faults you circled one through three, CONGRATULATIONS, you just discovered your spiritual stronghold. This stronghold is what is keeping you from living the abundant life God has promised you in John 10:10.

To begin the process of healing, we must first wage war on the stronghold we believe to be the most damaging to your relationship with God and your family. A stronghold you circled "1" will require your attention first and foremost than a stronghold you may have circled "3". If you indicated more than one stronghold, you're not alone. I had three strongholds. In case you're wondering why we tackle the biggest stronghold first, chances are your biggest stronghold is like a cancer, growing and feeding the others.

In order to defeat these strongholds, we need a battle plan. This battle plan has been created from my ten-year journey and has helped many men including myself. Why am I putting out my dirty laundry for the whole world to see? Because I believe God has a mission for me to help men who are hurting, and to give men a road map to help others overcome strongholds that are wrecking their lives. This battle plan has been tested and works. You must be willing to confront the sin head on with no looking back. Not only will you benefit from this move, the reward that comes from victory is worth the fight.

It is now time to resolve to make a difference in your life and most importantly those you love.

The Battle Plan

(1) **Confront Sin:** We just did this. Congratulations! By identifying our strongholds, we have our first small victory. Now we're going to need a weapon to defeat this stronghold. This is when we open our spiritual tool box. Your weapon is the Word of God.

> *"Put on the full armor of God, so that you will be able to stand firm against the schemes of the devil. For our struggle is not against flesh and blood, but against the spiritual forces of wickedness in heavenly places. Therefore, take up the full armor of God, so that you will be able to resist in the evil day, having done everything, to stand firm. Stand firm therefore, having girded your loins with truth, and having put on the breastplate of righteousness, having shod your feet with the preparation of the gospel of peace; in addition to all, taking up the shield of faith with which you will be able to extinguish all the flaming arrows of the evil one. And take the helmet of salvation, and the sword of the Spirit, which is the word of God."* Ephesians 6:11-17 (NASB)

This is a battle of the mind and spirit. The Bible is our weapon against spiritual warfare because it contains time-tested information that will give us freedom from our strongholds.

The Word of God

The Sword of the Spirit, which is the word of God, is the weapon that can inflict injury against the evil forces. The Word of God is what will defeat our strongholds. Remember in Chapter One we read that some people believe evil can somehow compete and win against good? This can only happen in your mind and only if you allow it. Satan and all his demons are absolutely no match for God. Evil can only win if we allow it to happen.

How the Word of God Works

Imagine our thoughts are in a gallon-size container. Right now, our mind is being filled with positive thoughts and knowledge. Our container will only hold one gallon of something whether it be positive or negative. As we are filling our minds with the positive, the negative thoughts are being flushed out. Since this is a spiritual battle, these evil forces are not going to give up so easy. Our sin nature slowly attempts to creep back in and flush out the positive thoughts.

When we stay in the Word daily, we keep replenishing the positive by flushing the negative back out. We must fill our minds with the Word of God. We should read no less than one chapter of our Bibles daily. If you have a King James version of the Bible and you find it hard to understand due to reading the thees and thous, I recommend a New King James Version, New International Version or an English Standard Version. There are also many Bible apps for your phone or device. I recommend you use the same Bible your pastor uses. This way when he quotes scripture, you will be able to follow along.

Take Notes

There is nothing wrong with writing notes in our Bibles. If we really want to see how the Bible is supposed to work, we should ask someone we trust at church to look at their Bible. I suspect is probably marked throughout. Some of the greatest men I know have Bibles held together with duct tape. This is not because they cannot afford a new Bible, but because there are so many personal notes in their Bible, and they don't want to lose it.

Spiritual warfare will always be in the mind and spirit. It's what we fill our heads with, our attitudes and our physical actions that will begin to change our thought process. If we invested as much time working against our strongholds as we used to cater to them, we are destined to win. "*That light shines in the darkness, and yet the darkness did not overcome it*" John 1:5 (NIV)

Make Quiet Time

We must infiltrate our minds with the Word of God. Read a chapter daily. The best way to do this is to pick out a time each day where only you and God spend time together. I know men who have actual prayer closets. In these closets is a light bulb, a chair and a Bible. These men lock themselves in the closet to pray and read. While I don't have a closet dedicated to this, I use my home office. Others make a cup of coffee and sit in their recliners or at their dining room tables. However we decide to do this, we must set aside a time when we spend one-on-one time with the word of God. We cannot allow anything to interfere with this time. Typically, an average quiet time takes about twenty minutes a day. Do you feel like you don't have twenty minutes a day to spare? Make time. Nothing can be more important than our personal time with God.

Prayer

Always start with prayer. Ask God to reveal something new each day and ask for His protection from the evil ones. Understand Satan is not going to like this new life change. He will come after us through noise, interruptions, responsibilities, technology, loud children, or whatever else can distract us. A very prominent pastor in my community gets in his truck and drives to a secluded area of the county every day for his quiet time so as not to be interrupted by noise. He says some of his best sermons came out of those times with God, his truck and his Bible.

The more we fill our minds with the Word of God, the less room there is left for the strongholds to occupy. There will be times we may read our Bibles and feel like nothing was accomplished, but down the road the Word from God will present itself. *"So shall my word be that goes forth from My mouth; It shall not return to Me void, But it shall accomplish what I please, And it shall prosper in the thing for which I sent it."* Isaiah 55:11 (NKJV). You will begin to notice small victories. The more we read, the more our subconscious is molded to the perspective of God.

As we begin to practice this good habit, we start to miss the "our time" with God. When we read the Bible, we feel ourselves drawing closer to God. (This is the gallon full of positives versus a gallon full of negatives.) God created us and desires a relationship with us. His favorite way of speaking to us is through His Word. When we pray we are speaking to God. How can we have a relationship with God if we don't speak with Him?

(2) **SEEK FORGIVENESS.** Confession. Men, where there is no confession, there is no healing. James 5:16 (NIV) says, "*Therefore confess your sins to each other and pray for each other so that you may be healed.*" It goes on to say, "*the prayer of a righteous man is powerful and effective.*" That righteous man this verse speaks of could be an accountability partner or someone within our circle of friends who possesses Godly wisdom.

So, who do we confess to?

Our first confession needs to be to God. It is Him we have offended the most. He has laid out a way for us to be in relationship with Him and we have politely declined. The great news is God already knows. That's why He put the story of the prodigal son as found in Luke 15:11-32. Now would be a good time to stop here in this book, pick up your Bible and read this story.

In this story where the father is running out to meet his son, that's God. He's the father in this story and the son is you. I've had some ask the question "if God already knows my sin, why do I have to confess it?" God wants your obedience. God wants you to place all of your cards on the table. Relationships struggle when one or both parties involved have secrets. Only when we trust Him with our secrets can He begin a mighty work in us. Just like in an Alcoholics Anonymous meeting (AA), men must stand up, state their name and admit publicly that they have an addiction. God says, "*My eyes are on all of their ways; they are not hidden from me, nor is their sin concealed from my eyes*" Jeremiah 16:17 (NIV). God has always known and admitting our sin means we are halfway there. He is just to forgive. All we have to do is repent and ask. "*He heals the brokenhearted and bandages their wounds*" Psalm 147:3 (NLT).

We also must confess to our wives. Now, before you fall out of your chair and start thinking she will divorce you, realize she probably already knows. I had an affair for three years and struggled with the right way to share this with my wife. If you really don't think she knows, and you are fearful of confessing to her, consult with your pastor or seek sound counseling from a professional Christian counselor. I truly believe if you don't confess to her, then you have not completed your process of repentance.

Our wives are our life partners. They have the right to know and we will not be free from the weight of guilt until we confess to them. Yes, I have seen marriages break up after confessing affairs. Sometimes when a wife sees her husband making changes for the betterment of his walk with Christ and their life as husband and wife, she often wants to work things out. Often this has to do with the spiritual maturity of the wife. Nonetheless, I still recommend consulting with a pastor or a Christian marriage counselor.

As the offender, we must ask God for help, to change our hearts so we can be free from the spiritual bondage that is keeping us from living the abundant life God has offered. Just a thought here: Why are we more afraid to confess our sin to our wives than to confess our sin before God? If we are, then there is a deeper lying issue regarding our relationship and fear of God.

Lastly, we have to tell our accountability partner. One of the greatest lies from hell is our misconception that men can do life on their own. We can't. Men need other men to support them throughout their journey through life. This is why I believe so strongly in a men's ministry. For every sin I have committed, there have been other men in my life to help me put the pieces back together again. They have held me when I've cried. They have called me out when I wouldn't listen. They have never left my side. (This is the very reason why I have the courage to write this book.) In Don Otis's book titled *Whisker Rubs*, he says, "God placed men in the lives of other men for the purpose to push them beyond what they think they can do, beyond their zones of comfort."

If we want to bring the darkness into the light, then we must confess our sins to God first and foremost, then to our wives and finally to our accountability partners. This will leave no place to hide for our strongholds. Then we will be one more step closer in the process of building a battle plan to confront our strongholds.

(3) Answer the call: Here I am, Lord.

"Here I am, Lord." We must commit to the teachings of God. We must be willing to do what every hero in the Bible has done by making the statement. Then we can watch what God will begin to do in your life. God has a plan for every one of His creations. God desires to take our mess and turn it into a message. What better way to remind evil that God is still in control? We must do our part by opening our hearts to God. If you have never accepted Jesus into your heart, all that is required is for you to remain where you are and pray. Submit to Jesus that you know you are a sinner. Confess to Jesus that you know He died for your sin on the cross, and ask Him to save you. Yes, it is that simple. Don't allow evil to try to convince you there is more than simply asking God for forgiveness and accepting Him into your heart. Salvation is a free gift and you can do nothing to earn this gift. Otherwise it is not a gift.

Our sin has already been placed at the foot of the cross. *"For by grace you have been saved through faith, and not of yourselves; it is the gift of God, not of works, lest anyone should boast."* Ephesians 2:8-9 (NKJV). If we are already saved and our strongholds have kept us from living according to God's will, we are not alone and it's not too late to repent. Remember the story of the prodigal son? Jesus loves us and wants us to come back to Him. We must resolve to confront our sin, seeking forgiveness and to answer His call. *"Be strong and be of good courage, do not fear nor be afraid of them; for the Lord your God, He is the one who goes with you. He will not leave you or forsake you."* Deuteronomy 31:6 (NKJV).

Looking Ahead

In these next ten chapters we will address each stronghold individually. We will discuss their origins and offer a battle plan on how to confront and defeat each stronghold. I ask that you read each chapter whether it applies to your life or not. I guarantee we all know a man who is dealing with one of these strongholds. If not, just wait.

Each chapter builds upon each other with insight and personal stories that should be helpful. At the end of each chapter there is a series of questions that will be helpful for larger or small group study.

1) In what area of your life have you seen where God is a God of second chances? _____

_____

_____

2) What is your spiritual stronghold? _____

_____

_____

3) Do you have more than one spiritual stronghold? _____

_____

_____

4) If so name your other strongholds _____

_____

_____

5) Do you read your Bible? _____

If not, please write the date you will begin._____

6) Do you have an accountability partner? _____

_____

_____

7) When and what time will you have your quiet time with God?

_____

_____

_____

_____

Photo by Kevin Carden

CHAPTER THREE

Addictions

Psychology Today Describes an addiction as "a condition that results when a person ingests a substance (alcohol, cocaine, nicotine, etc.) or engages in an activity (gambling, sex, shopping, etc.) that can be pleasurable but the continuation of which becomes compulsive and interferes with ordinary responsibilities and concerns such as work, relationships or health." People who have developed an addiction may not be aware that their behavior is out of control and causing problems for themselves and others.

Addictions can be physical and/or psychological. Physical addiction is a biological state in which the body adapts to the presence of a drug so that drug no longer has the same effect, also known as tolerance. This changes our physical chemistry and cannot be fixed with just willpower. As in heroin addiction, while willpower is important, they shouldn't try to get clean without a physician or other professional help because the withdrawals could be fatal. Psychological addiction is the overreaction by the brain to certain urges and feelings, but our biology stays the same. This would be like a man who feels a strong inclination to look at pornography everytime he picks up his phone or logs into his computer. His body will be fine without it, but his mind is telling him he needs it.

While professionals debate on whether addiction is a mental illness or a physical disease, it is clear that addiction is a disorder of the brain's reward system. There is a wide range of genetic and environmental risk factors for developing an addiction that vary across the population. Roughly half of an individual's risk for developing an addiction is derived from genetics. The other half is derived from the environment. Anyone can become an addict under the right circumstances.

I made a point to stay away from alcohol due to the alcohol abuse suffered from both sides of my family. Epidemiological studies estimate that genetic factors account for forty to sixty percent of the risk factors for alcoholism. Determining the origin of the addiction in our personal lives is our first step in confronting and defeating this illness.

I am not a professional counselor or a college trained professor on the issue of addiction, but I have seen enough addictions in others and personally to know that until we treat an addiction as an illness, we will never gain an upper hand on this stronghold. It does not require a doctorate degree to understand what addictions are doing to our families and ourselves. We would be hard pressed to find a family that has not dealt with, or is dealing with, some form of addiction.

Addictions may be something as socially acceptable as food or could be as taboo as cocaine. Either way an addiction is a stronghold, and there is only one way to defeat this illness. The first step is to have a head-on collision with reality. We must admit we have a problem. Then we must get help. Many times, our pride is a major contributing factor for the continuation of an addiction.

When I was in my teen years, my mother was the greatest mom a person could have. I cannot say the same for much of my younger life, my mother was addicted to prescription drugs and alcohol. I will never forget when I was young boy, I walked out of my room to find once again my parents and family members drinking and partying. This time it had gotten so far out of hand, none of the adults realized there was a young boy (me), sitting in the crowd as they watched an 8mm film with explicit scenes. My father had no idea as he was partying in another part of the house. I had become so uncomfortable and upset seeing images such as this for the first time in my life, that I rose from the dark room and ran to my bedroom uncontrollably crying. I knew something inside of me had changed forever. My father noticed me as I ran by. I looked at him and yelled "Either they go, or I go." Where I would go, I had no idea, but never in my life had I felt so unprotected and unsafe. The images on that film stole my innocents.

I couldn't have imagined my father's response. He immediately entered the dark room, turned over and slammed the stereo system and crashed the projector which contained the explicit scenes. As complete silence filled the house and everyone looking on, he said, "Everyone, out of my house now." That evening would also be the first time in my life I felt loved by my father.

I stood by as everyone collected their liquor bottles and other belongings and left the house with not one word uttered. As the house cleared my father who was a man of few words turned to my mother and said, "This stops now." It was that same evening I saw my mother confront her addictions. I watched my mother demonstrate genuine love for her husband and her son as she without hesitation began dumping drugs down the toilet and pouring dozens of beer bottles down the kitchen sink.

That hot summer night in South Georgia planted four distinct seeds within my young mind. (1) Being exposed to sex on an 8mm film projector launched an almost forty-year battle with my own sexual stronghold. (2) That evening unleashed an anger inside of me I had never felt. (3) I realized alcohol was something I did not want to control my life. (4) I believe this very day the love my mother demonstrated towards me by dumping her addictions down the drain gave me the courage to confront my own struggles and eventually lead to writing this book. Up until her death in 1997 I thought my mother had taken on these addictions all by herself and won. I did not realize until a few years ago that it was at this very time my mother became active in a local church.

Is Addiction a Sin?

Addicts feel as if they are trapped and out of control. They feel like they are in bondage, enslaved, stuck and without hope for freedom or escape. Something is controlling them. It tells them how to live, think and feel. Sin is anything that separates us from a holy God. It is a failure to conform to the law of God either in action or attitude. When it comes to addictions, most people do not consider the fact that an addiction is also sin.

> *"Then one of them, a lawyer, asked Him a question,*
> *testing Him, and saying, "Teacher, which is the great*

commandment in the law?" Jesus said to him, "You shall love the Lord your God with all your heart, with all your soul, and with all your mind.' This is the first and great commandment. And second is like it: 'You shall love your neighbor as yourself.' On these two commandments hang all the Law and the Prophets." Matthew 22:35-40 (NKJV)

Jesus desires to be the center of our lives. "Loving your neighbor as yourself" was the proverbial stake in the ground that helped my mother overcome her addictions. It was a body of believers who loved on her and walked with her during some very dark times. In the year that followed that horrific evening, my mother became the greatest mom a boy could ask for and my father became my hero. We became a family.

Mom was the coolest mother any teenage boy could have. She was like a guardian angel to many of my friends in times of teenage difficulty. She was simply known as "Mom Stuckey". It was also during this time my father began to lead his family by example.

I share this story so those of us who struggle with addictions can realize it's never too late to regain our lives. These were difficult times for me and my family in the early 70s. While there were sinful seeds planted, I see how God was in the business of taking my mess and turning it into a message. In the case of struggling with addictions, there is no question we must seek help, but we cannot receive a complete understanding and healing of our struggles without the intervention of a loving, just, and holy God.

Before Christ saved me, many men have sought me out for advice when dealing with addictions. I credit this to my openness and transparency about the struggles me and my family went through because of addiction. People like to know that they are not alone when it comes to addictions and their consequences.

It was not until God saved me at the age of forty-nine years old did I begin to truly understand these gifts. I realized then that God had a purpose for my life, and had given me the spiritual gifts in which to work His purpose out in my life. What we don't understand is regardless of where we are in our lives whether a drug addict or a successful accountant, God has a purpose for each one of us. We will never understand that purpose until we began seeking Him for answers and making Him the most important thing in our lives as mentioned in Matthew 22:35-40.

I have often wondered what our community would look like if everyone was a believer and understood their spiritual gifts. Unfortunately, we'll have to wait until Heaven to realize the significance of a love such as this. For us as individuals, we do not have to wait for heaven. We can realize our calling simply by first asking Christ into our hearts. Whether we have yet to do this or have already been saved by God's free gift of salvation, all we have to do is put Christ into the center of our lives, begin to seek His will for our lives and watch as Christ begins to move in ways never thought possible.

Making God The Center not our Addiction

Imagine how different our lives would be if we spent as much time studying His word rather than being consumed with our addictions. When we focus on Christ, He will give you a desire to open your spiritual toolbox and read the Bible.

Throughout my life I have never had the patience to read a book. My laziness and lack of desire to read was a very big reason why I was unable to accomplish my dream of playing college football. I was a good enough athlete to be noticed by schools, but not good enough that anyone was willing to look past my poor study habits. I carried this bad habit into adulthood. The only book I have ever read as a young man was John Madden's "Hey wait a minute, I wrote a book". Once I was saved, I had a passion to learn who was this man named Jesus who died for someone as sinful as me.

I'll never forget the day God rescued me (January 8, 2006). The very next day I took a day off from work to travel to various book stores trying to find a book about Jesus. I needed to know who Jesus was as well as His history and the history leading up to the beginning of His story. The old King James Version Bible my grandmother gave me when I was six years old would not do the job because I did not understand the terminology (*thee* and *thou*). That's not how we talk in the deep south.

As a "baby" Christian I was not aware that the Bible was translated in a way so that I could understand it's teachings. I had no idea the New International Version or the New King James Version existed for people like me who didn't have a degree in early British Literature. I had to create a formula which would help me check and balance my reservations about why there are so many different versions of the Bible.

For the next eight months I sat in my recliner with a King James version on my end table, a New King James version in my lap and a New International version on a t.v. tray. I compared verse by verse until I reached the book of Revelation 22:21, which is the last verse in each Bible. I was amazed when I realized I had just read three Bibles front to back in just eight months. Then it hit me: *"Blessed is he who reads and those who hear the words of this prophecy and keep those things which are written in it; for the time is near"* Revelation 1:3 (NKJV). After I read the Bible, I felt a sense of wisdom. I found it amazing how when things in my life would be out of sync, how the words from certain scriptures would come to me when I needed them most. This was a reminder that God was always with me. I realized every person walking the face of this earth could experience the same comfort I had when times were tough by just simply reading His word.

I have now read the Bible eleven times since 2006. I have been asked why I have read the Bible so many times. I have read the Bible for many purposes: to fulfill my need for knowledge, to understand the history of mankind, and to understand my own lineage much further back than when the first Stuckey stepped foot on American soil in 1600. (Our lineage goes back to our grandfather Adam in the book of Genesis.) Most importantly I read the Bible to feel closer to Jesus. This helps me to make Jesus the center of my life instead of my addiction. This freedom is available to everyone.

The Reward of the Word

When we read the Word daily we are better connected to God. When we don't stay in the Word, we revert back to our old ways which always get us in trouble. When we do not read His word our problems in life appear larger. The Bible gives us everyday tools in which to maneuver through life with a better understanding and comfort.

This is why I call the Bible a spiritual tool box. Not only does our spiritual toolbox help fix things in our own lives, it also helps us to encourage others to repair things in their lives. God wired us to live life together, this is why we all have spiritual gifts.

> *"Having then gifts differing according to the grace that is given to us, let us use them; if prophecy, let us prophesy in proportion to our faith; or ministry, let us use it in our ministering; he who teaches, in teaching; he who exhorts, in exhortation; he who gives, with liberality; he who leads, with diligence; he who shows mercy, with cheerfulness."* Romans 12:6-8 (NKJV).

I have heard many unbelievers say they have never felt the presence of God. This is because they have never invited God into their lives. *"Behold, I stand at the door and knock. If anyone hears My voice and opens the door, I will come in to him and dine with him, and he with Me."* Revelation 3:20 (NKJV). Others have said they have never heard from God. The truth is God is always speaking, but we can't hear from God when we don't listen or when we allow the situations of the world to drown out that still small voice. Psalm 46:10 (NKJV) says *"Be still, and know I am God."* When I am asked about discerning God's voice, I often share noise, in general, today is a deterrent of God's voice. We are encouraged as Christians to find a quiet place to study in order to block out the noise, so that we can hear God's voice.

All through scripture people have heard God's voice in many ways. Ezekiel 43:2 and Revelation 1:15 says His voice was like the sound of many waters. Revelation 1:10 and Revelation 4:1 says He has a loud voice like the sound of a trumpet. Hebrews 12:26 says He has a voice that shook the earth. Job 37:2 says God's voice is like the sound of thunder. God speaks in a way which will best get our attention. The most popular way in which Christians like to speak of God's voice is found in the book of 1 Kings 19:11-13 (NKJV). This is the story in which the prophet Elijah hears God's voice.

> *"Then He said, "Go out, and stand on the mountain before the Lord." And behold, the Lord passed by, and a great and strong wind tore into the mountains and broke the*

rocks in pieces before the Lord, but the Lord was not in the wind; and after the wind an earthquake, but the Lord was not in the earthquake, and after the earthquake a fire, but the Lord was not in the fire; and after the fire a still small voice. So it was when Elijah heard it, that he wrapped his face in his mantle and went out and stood in the entrance of the cave. Suddenly a voice came to him, and said, "What are you doing here, Elijah?"

What does God's voice sound like? Any way He wants it to sound.

There are some Pastors who preach that God does not speak today. I strongly disagree. I first heard God speak on December 1, 2007 while driving south on I-95 headed for home from a family conference in Wake Forest, North Carolina. It came to me as if instant knowledge. A thought pressed into my mind which contained a statement "Go start a softball league that will glorify Me." My first thought was to question softball. It was through softball in Jacksonville Beach, Florida where an affair of three years began. Everything I did through softball was to glorify myself, and back then, I was willing to do anything to accomplish my goal. I stepped on feelings along the way and completely ruined my reputation, as well as almost destroy my family in the process.

My reasoning for moving to Fernandina Beach was to get away from this bad situation in order to rebuild my family and I had felt that softball had to go, too. I'll never forget the moment when I walked in the door and explained to my wife "God wants me to start a softball league." The good news for me was my wife was saved that very morning which I believe saved me from a frying pan upside my head. Out of this still small voice and for over ten years now the Family Driven Softball League has flourished. Dads, moms and teens are enjoying a recreational activity together as are many other folks from many different churches and denominations. Since its inception in 2009, other Christian sports leagues have inquired about how we keep this league successfully going while there are so many other "church leagues" which are failing. I tell them we keep Jesus first and pray over every game.

The second time I heard the voice of God was on May 5, 2014. At a revival at my former home church, Pastor Darryl Bellar was speaking of the life of Gideon from the book of Judges Chapters 6 through 8. I was in a very dark place in my life and was desiring to hear from God. Suddenly I heard a voice state "Ernie, I am not done with you yet." Once again as if instant knowledge hit my mind, I began a journey that led to the birth of the Christian Men's Association of North Florida. Today this ministry comprises of roughly fifty men from an average of eleven different churches who enjoy fellowship, meals and round table discussions together. We also have a group of women who gather at the same time in our home for prayer for each man who is in attendance. The focus of the group is to promote men's ministry in the church, as well as helping men be the best fathers, husbands and Christians we can be.

My reason for sharing this information on whether God still speaks today is simply because when an addict cries out for help they need to know that God hears them.

So those who do not believe God speaks today, I offer the scripture as found in John 10:27 (NKJV) where Jesus says *"My sheep hear my voice, and I know them, and they follow Me."* For those who say they cannot hear the voice of God, whether a believer or non-believer, I would suggest getting rid of all the noise, finding a quiet place and listen. Yes, it is that simple. If the gift of salvation is so simple, then why isn't hearing the voice of God as simple? Yes, we must be careful to discern His voice from our own thoughts, as well as the evil ones attempting to mislead. I maintain a great way to know whether God is speaking to you is to look for and follow results.

God will never ask you to do something that encourages sin or cannot be edified by your spiritual toolbox. There are no new stories being created to add to scripture, only situations where God can be glorified and produces heavenly results for the betterment of a relationship with Him. God will open and close doors depending on where He wants you to go.

There are times God chooses not to speak for reasons we do not understand. Sometimes God will not speak because His answer is simply no. Other times God does not speak because He already knows our intentions are for personal gain or are not in the best interest of ourselves. Regardless of His intentions for not speaking, He still hears our prayers. If a non-believer asks God to speak to him and God does not speak, then perhaps, they are asking with the wrong motives. Regardless of a non-believer's arrogance or pride, God does not have to speak to anyone. Just because God allows us to think we are in control doesn't mean we are. The bottom line is God is God, and He does what He knows is best.

Get Help

In the case of addictions, we must without hesitation seek help. The longer we put off seeking help, the stronger our brain desires the pleasure. Once we realize we have an addiction, we must go on the offensive. We must surround ourselves with Godly men who will put us on the right path and walk beside us. Those who only claim to be our friends will not help. Those who truly love us will do whatever they can to help.

When I was in the middle of my affair back in Jacksonville Beach, there were others whom I thought were my friends. Some of my biggest supporters were also having affairs or were living an adulteress lifestyle. I realized the only way I could get out of my adulteress lifestyle was to remove myself and my family from the situation. This was why we moved to Fernandina Beach. It was absolutely one of the hardest things I've ever had to do, not to mention the burden I had put on my wife and children. None of the people who were involved in my life back then, are my friends today. Instead God brought men of accountability into my life. Today there are men whom I would go to the ends of the earth to protect because I know in my heart, they would do the same way for me.

Your Battle Plan for defeating addictions:

(1) Confront the sin

One of the hardest steps we must take is to first admit we have an addiction. Once we realize we have an addiction we must then determine the origin of the sin. We must first determine whether our addiction is from an environmental perspective or from genetics.

Environment - If we find that our addiction is derived from our environment, we must take immediate action and remove ourselves from the environment that promotes this unhealthy lifestyle.

Sometimes this requires moving from a particular neighborhood or some change of location. Sometimes this requires choosing different friends or even jobs. We often blame money as an excuse for being unable to relocate or change jobs.

A lack of money is nothing more than an excuse for not making a healthy lifestyle change. If you were living in an area where the soil in your yard was causing your children to be sick, you would not hesitate to find a way to move your family to a safer location. Your spiritual toolbox speaks of loving yourself enough to make healthy lifestyle changes. *"To acquire wisdom is to love oneself; people who cherish understanding will prosper"* Proverbs 19:8 (NLT). *"For no one hates his own body but feeds and cares for it, just as Christ cares for the church"* Ephesians 5:29 (NLT).

Genetics – Genetics is a study of heredity. Heredity is a biological process where one parent passes down certain genes to their children. Every child inherits genes from both parents and these genes express certain traits. This is why when you visit the doctor they ask for your family's medical history. Your genetics can also determine your tendency to suffer from other addictions such as alcohol abuse. The Bible speaks of the generational curse. Regarding the generational curse, God is clear on this subject.

> *"You shall not bow down to them nor serve them, For I, the Lord am a jealous God, visiting the iniquity of the fathers upon the children to the third and fourth generations of those who hate Me, but showing mercy to thousands, of those who love me and keep my commandments."* Deuteronomy 5:9-10 (NKJV).

God has also forgiven men their trespass and removing the generational curse *"Yet you say, 'Why should the son not bear the guilt of the father?' Because the son has done what is lawful and right, and has kept all My statutes and observed them, he shall surely live."* Ezekiel 18:19 (NKJV). God has blessed us with many ways to confront the stronghold of addiction, but finding the right one (or ones) is critical to our success.

(2) Seek forgiveness:

In order to begin the healing process, we must seek forgiveness from those we have hurt, and we must also forgive ourselves. The Bible speaks of repentance. Repentance means to flee or to make a complete 180 degree turn from our sin. The confession of sin is required in order to receive atonement and forgiveness. To repent means not only to turn away, but to demonstrate true brokenness for the offense. Repentance is not asking the Lord for forgiveness with intent to sin again, but rather honest, regretful acknowledgment of sin. When we ask God for forgiveness, He is willing and just to forgive. In order to purge ourselves from addictions we must take immediate action against the addiction. In the case of chemical abuse, medical treatment and professional counseling is required.

(3) Answer the call:

> *"Come to Me, all you who labor and are heavy laden, and I will give you rest. Take My yoke upon you and learn from Me, for I am gentle and lowly in heart, and you will find rest for your souls. For My yoke is easy and My burden is light"* Matthew 11:28-30 (NKJV).

I love this analogy Jesus uses in this verse. A yoke is a wooden cross piece that is fastened over the necks of two animals and attached to a plow or cart they pull together. In this case we are one who is attached to the yoke, but Jesus is attached along with us as we pull the plow of life together.

As I have said several times in this chapter, in the case of chemical addictions such as alcohol abuse or drug abuse, we must act immediately without hesitation. Do not give thought as to whether you should or should not seek medical help or counseling. Reach out to someone who will hold you accountable and ask them to drive you to your doctor's appointments if necessary. If you must, have this same person call and schedule doctors' appointments and ask them under no circumstances to allow you to back out of the appointment. That inner voice that is saying "you're fine" is the spiritual warfare as mentioned in Chapter One. We must work to find a way to defeat this.

Regardless of your addiction, remember you are suffering from an illness that is controlling your every move. Hesitation gives in to procrastination. Procrastination itself will become a living and breathing entity if we give in to it.

Finally get in the word of God. Open your Bible and set your mind on thoughts and words that bring healing, not destruction. You must resolve to get well. Pray to Him and ask Him for help and strength.

> "Do not love the world or things in the world. If anyone loves the world, the love of the Father is not in him. For all that is in the world, the lust of the flesh, the lust of the eyes, and the pride of life, is not of the Father but is of the world. And the world is passing away, and the lust of it; but he who does the will of God abides forever" 1 John 2:15-17 (NKJV).

For those who are dealing with addictions, you are not alone. Never forget one of Satan's chief plans is to isolate you in order to make you feel alone, or that you are the only one going through this addiction. When he gets you alone, he then infiltrates your mind with pleasures of the flesh which is a direct attack on the brain's reward system. There is no such thing as failure when it comes to God. God doesn't know how to fail. "Jesus looked at them intently and said, 'Humanly speaking, it is impossible. But with God everything is possible'" Matthew 19:26 (NLT).

Photo by Kevin Carden

1) Have you or anyone you know suffered from an addiction?

_____
_____
_____
_____

2) Do you believe the addiction mentioned in question one is derived from the environment?_____ Genetics?_____
Explain:_____

_____
_____
_____
_____

3) How do you make God a priority in your life? _____

_____
_____
_____
_____

4) When is the last time you've used your spiritual tool box? _____

_____
_____
_____
_____

5) Do you believe God still speaks today?
Example:_____

_____
_____
_____
_____

6) Which of the following do you believe to be most effective when helping an addict?
Medical help: _____
Professional counseling: _____
Spiritual help: _____

All of the above: _____

Why?_____

_____

_____

_____

_____

7) For anyone in need of help from an addiction, how soon should they seek help?

Now? _____

Within days? _____

Within weeks? _____

Why?_____

_____

_____

_____

_____

CHAPTER FOUR

Anger

The number one stronghold that has consumed much of my life has been anger. What is anger and where does it come from?

Anger can be hereditary like many other disorders and conditions. Our emotions are controlled by hormones and chemicals in our bodies and if those are unbalanced, then we can "fly off the handle" without much thought. Anger can also be a learned behavior. How did our dads react to stress? What did we see from our brothers, teachers, and coaches? If anger was the answer to stressful situations and that was modeled for us at a young age, then we can assume that is how we are supposed to be.

Anger is not just an *either/or*, but can be a *both/and*. Christian counselors report that fifty percent of people who come in for counseling have problems dealing with anger. In my personal studies, I find anger to be the contributing factor for other issues, such as fear, lust, insecurities and depression.

Anger is an emotion

Everyone deals with anger. How we deal with it and to what intensity we allow it to heighten is what makes us different. There are doctors, physiologists and behavioral scientists who spend a great deal of their lives trying to explain certain theories of anger. People today are spending vast amounts of money trying to find answers to their anger issues, and some theories are constantly leading them down dead-end roads. This is one of the reasons why I believe we need a more common-sense approach to so many of our problems today. I am not a scientist, but I do believe that rather than constantly looking for new ways to fix ageless problems, perhaps we should reintroduce time-tested remedies as well as look for answers in our spiritual toolbox.

For example, some parents today are using drugs for their overactive children. I have no doubt this is a necessary drug for some. WebMD.com states the medication known as Adderall is used to lessen the "Can't sit still" behaviors in children and it improves the child's ability to concentrate and learn. This works for some, but what about the child who concentrates better when the body is introduced to more activity? Can't we agree this might be a better place to start? Regarding anger, an average person will go through no less than fifteen potential anger issues per day. How we respond to these anger issues may very well determine our levels of stress and longevity of life.

There are two anger models, and knowing their triggers, as well as our personal management skills will help us in defeating this battle of the mind. Before we discuss medications with our doctors, let's discuss why we get angry, where anger comes from, and the two models of anger.

Generational - Like generational addiction discussed in our previous chapter, generational anger is passed down from the spirit of the parent to the spirit of the child. You must understand the generational curse is not an Old Testament folklore, but a very real continuation of heredity. Have you ever witnessed a family where a father has a problem controlling his anger? You may also notice their children has the same traits. There is a very good chance the grandparent suffered from anger issues as well. God says in the book of Exodus

> "Keeping mercy for thousands, forgiving iniquity and transgression and sin, by no means clearing the guilty, visiting (punishing), the iniquity of the fathers upon the children and the children's children to the third and fourth generation." Exodus 34:7 (NKJV).

Although anger is an emotion, this stronghold can be passed along through spiritual bondage. Further proof of this statement can be found in people who are adopted. Their adoptive parents will not have the same trait as an adopted child, but it can be found in their birth parents such as family illness, mental problems, persistent irrational fears and depression.

Learned behavior - Like it or not children are like a sponge. They take in everything and copy what they see. Children pick up our bad habits. "Do as I say, not as I do" didn't work when our parents said it to us, do we think it will work from us to our kids? Think to yourself of certain good and bad habits that you may have, like using foul language, eating cookies before bedtime, watching western movies. My father had these habits, and now so do I.

Although generational anger and learned anger seem to be the same from its description, it is important to understand how we obtain this emotion so we can better plan our method of attack. For instance possessing generational anger may explain how we get angry, but have no way to compartmentalize it. We tend to get angry and stay angry with no reason as to why. Possessing anger from a learned behavior explains why we sometimes resort to physical retaliation. In my personal studies, I have seen those who resort to physical abuse is because it was modeled to them as a child. A child would watch his father physically harm his mother when the argument reaches a boiling point. The child grows up only to retaliate in the same manner with his wife when an argument reaches an impasse.

Generational anger seems to be more prominent in those who lash out in a non-physical retaliation. They seem to carry a grudge longer, or they tend to quietly and methodically plan out a retaliation such as mental abuse. Anger exhibited through physical anguish may very well come from a learned behavior, whereas someone who exhibits mental anguish may very well come from a generational behavior. There are many like me who show characteristics of both.

A very popular verse in the book of Proverbs says, "*Train a child in the way he should go and when he is old, he will not depart from it*" Proverbs 22:6 (NKJV). This works in reverse as well. Our children watch our every move. If we as men treat our wives as second-class citizens, you can rest assured there is a greater chance our sons will pick up on this bad habit and do the same to their wives when they are older. Think about where did you learn to deal with anger? Who modeled that behavior for you?

In either case, breaking the chain of anger requires deliberate steps in defeating this stronghold. As with every stronghold, we must first determine the severity of anger in our lives.

Is it a mere passing thought?

Since we know an average person goes through at least fifteen anger issues per day, we know that each situation will have different levels in which to deal. As discussed in Chapter Two "a passing thought" is merely a sudden idea. This thought will leave our minds almost as swiftly as it has entered it. If something causes you to become angry but you dispel it without further consideration, then obviously this is not considered a spiritual stronghold. Having passing thoughts of anger means you are no different than anyone else.

A Bad habit?

Do you tend to get angry often? Like other emotions, anger is experienced throughout our bodies, as well as in our minds. There is a complex series of physiological events that occur as we become angry. In our brain there is a structure called the Amygdala. This structure is responsible for identifying threats to our well-being. This structure sends out an alarm to our body causing us to go into personal protection mode. The Cortex (the part of our brain responsible for thought and reason), can determine if the threat is actually real. God wired our brain to cause us to react before we consider the consequences of our actions. This is the mechanism that gives mankind the instinct for getting angry. Our anger instinct does not come from animals.

For some of us, our reaction to this instinct is harder to control. Using the Cortex part of our brain in times of anger is something we must learn how to do. We can teach ourselves to be more alert when our defense mechanism (Amygdala), begins to respond. When situations of anger arise, we can teach ourselves to immediately respond with thought and reason. Remember, it only becomes sin when we begin to entertain the thought. We can overcome our bad habit of getting angry by being more conscience of our anger triggers.

Consuming Anger

If anger consumes who we are then we have a spiritual stronghold with anger. We seem to get angry often. We exclude the fact that getting angry this often is contrary to living a healthy life. In time our anger starts to affect our body to the point where depression will begin to set. If it sounds like I have experience in this it's because I do. I realized my anger was a stronghold when something simple or accidental would happen, and I would leap to uncontrolled rage.

Many years back I used to coach girls fastpitch softball. My daughter, Amber, was a very good player. When she was twelve years old, she decided to become a pitcher. She had good speed for her age, but her ball control needed work. We would travel to the local softball park with a bucket of softballs. I would dump the balls at her feet at the pitching rubber and from forty feet away sit on the bucket in a catcher's position holding my glove in position for her to throw. I realized I had gotten older and that my reaction time was not what it used to be when Amber pitched a drop ball and I missed. The ball hit squarely between my legs and I was immediately in extreme pain.

About five minutes went by and the pain subsided, when suddenly I noticed all four surrounding ball fields were pin-drop silence. Looking up I noticed every child, coach and parent are staring at me with their mouths wide open. Those five minutes of walking off the pain included loud outbursts of foul language. In the moment the anger that consumed me allowed for me to not even realize what I had done. As we grabbed the gear and slowly walked out to the car in embarrassment, one of my coaching friends looked at me and said "Dude, I don't even know what some of those words mean." The worst realization for me was that my daughter had heard so many of my anger outbursts, this one didn't even affect her.

When Professional Help is Required

When anger becomes rage is when we need help. My wife used to tell me I could get so angry that I would zone out or go into another place. Not a day goes by that do I not feel the sorrow for allowing my anger to consume so much of my life. I realize that God is a God of second chances. If you find yourself having moments of rage, I beg you to get professional counseling or seek out your pastor and address this matter with him. Do not delay. You may have already experienced moments of rage where you have done something you regret. The good news is, it's not too late. But you must get help for this stronghold before you end up hurting someone you love or hurting yourself.

Is Anger a Sin?

Not always. Anger can be used for good or to glorify God. If the emotion of anger moves you to protect someone from harm, or to right a wrong or a retaliation to a wrong, this type of anger is not a sin.

Did you know Jesus got angry? Jesus lived a perfect and sinless life but got angry twice. Jesus cleared the Temple of the money changers and the animal sellers. He showed great emotion and anger.

> "Then Jesus went into the temple of God and drove out all those who bought and sold in the temple and overturned the tables of the money changers and the seats of those who sold doves. And He said to them 'It is written, my house shall be called a house of prayer', but you have made it a den of thieves" Matthew 21:12-13 (NKJV).

His anger was justified because at its root was concern for God's holiness and worship. Jesus took quick and decisive action. You can read more about these events in Mark 11:15-18 and John 2:13-22.

The second time Jesus became angry was in the synagogue of Capernaum when the Pharisees refused to answer His questions.

> "And he entered the synagogue again, and a man was there who had a withered hand. So they watched Him

closely, whether He would heal him on the Sabbath, so that they might accuse Him. And He said to the man who had the withered hand, 'Step forward.' Then He said to them, 'Is it lawful on the Sabbath to do good or to do evil, to save a life or to kill?' But they kept silent. And when He had looked around at them with anger, being grieved by the hardness of their hearts, He said to the man, 'Stretch out your hand.' And he stretched it out, and his hand was restored as whole as the other" Mark 3:1-5 (NKJV).

In order to confront sinful anger, we must create a battle plan. Reviewing your chart as found in Chapter Two, if you circled anger numbers one through three, the time is now to wage war against this spiritual stronghold.

Confront the sin

Our first step in defeating this stronghold is to confront the sin. We must first admit to ourselves we have a problem with anger. We now know where sinful anger comes from and whether it is generational or a learned behavior.

Breaking the generational curse can only be done through repentance and forgiveness. *"Yet you say, 'Why should the son not bear the guilt of the father?' Because the son has done what is lawful and right, and has kept all My statutes and observed them, He shall surely live"* Ezekiel 18:19 (NKJV). When we truly repent and ask God for forgiveness, He is just to forgive. When this happens *"Christ has redeemed us from the curse of the law, having become a curse for us (for it is written, "Cursed is everyone who hangs on a tree")*, Galatians 3:13 (NKJV). Jesus took care of all sin on that tree. Without Him there is no forgiveness of the generational curse. We must break the chain of the generational curse, or leave our heredity of sinful anger for unknown generations.

We must change our learned behavior of sinful anger by focusing more on the cortex of our brain which is responsible for thought and reason. We must learn to think twice before responding negatively. One way to help master our mind is to not put ourselves in situations where our anger can be aroused. We must focus more on the pleasant things of this world and less on trigger points like stress and fatigue. Proper rest and exercise will help alleviate stress which in turn reduces thoughts of anger.

Our most prized possession to help us with our anger issues is our spiritual toolbox. Filling our minds with the things of holiness will help flush out our tendency to get angry. We must focus on changing our way of thinking. We must ask ourselves what we think about during the course of the day. What can we do to reduce our fifteen anger issues per day and continue to work towards the nonexistence of these issues.

If we do not break this chain, our children will most assuredly follow in our footsteps. Spending more quiet time with our Bibles will help break the chain of sinful anger. We must focus on changing our thought process by making our lives a living sacrifice to God.

> *"I beseech you therefore, brethren, by the mercies of God, that you present your bodies a living sacrifice, holy, acceptable to God, which is your reasonable service. And do not be conformed to this world, but be transformed by the renewing of your mind, that you may prove what is good and acceptable and perfect will of God"* Romans 12:1-2 (NKJV).

Seek forgiveness

We must ask forgiveness for our anger. Even though God knows our every thought, He desires communication and a personal relationship with us. God is not this great and mighty spirit who lives in the heavenly realm passing judgment on everyone. God is a loving God. The reason God created mankind in the first place was so He could have fellowship with His creation. Does God get angry? Is God a jealous God? The Bible tells us yes on both. Do we get angry when a child or a loved one gets out of line? Are we jealous for a child's love when they pay more attention to things we know are not good for them?

We are God's children so why is it considered strange when He says He is a jealous God or an angry God. *"My son, do not despise the chastening of the Lord, Nor be discouraged when you are rebuked by Him. For whom the Lord loves He chastens and scourges every son whom He receives"* Hebrews 12:5:6 (NKJV). God never becomes angry from a sinful perspective. One of the questions I field from atheists often is "If there is a God, how can God be called a loving God when He goes around condemning everyone and allows such terrible things to happen to His people?" The answer is simple: we tend to see things with our own eyes and from our own perspective rather than view this world from God's perspective and through God's eyes. God did not hand us over to evil, we purchased it for ourselves with our actions. We are the ones who walked away from God. God never walked away from us. We throw Him out of our schools and then question Him when a deranged person walks into the schools and shoot children.

We ask the question "where is the justice for the innocent children who were shot." My response is to tell people that once you gain entry into the most wonderful, beautiful place your eyes have ever seen, a place where moths and rust cannot destroy, a place where there is no more sickness or sin and you're in the constant presence of a just and loving God, would you want to come back to earth? When an innocent child dies, they go to Heaven. The best we can imagine is this place called Earth. There is so much more awaiting us. Those children are in a beautiful place, and they are okay.

Bad things happen to good people because we live in a sinful world. Yes, God allows it, we just simply don't understand the reasons. One thing I do know, it is okay to be mad at God. He can handle it. *"And we know that all things work together for good to those who love God, to those who are called according to His purpose."* Romans 8:28 (NKJV).

Why do bad things happen to good people. It really comes down to our trust we put in God in every circumstance of our lives. Does He not have a better plan for us?

> *"For My thoughts are not your thoughts, neither are your ways My ways, declares the Lord. For as the heavens are higher than the earth, so are My ways higher than your ways and My thoughts than your thoughts."* Isaiah 55:8-9 (ESV).

If only the unbeliever would take time to open the word of God and read it from a perspective of seeking knowledge rather than looking for a reason to debate the scripture, they would clearly see the answers to their questions.

"We love Him because He first loved us." 1 John 4:19 (NKJV). Of all scripture written in the Bible, this scripture speaks the loudest to me. How can God love someone who is as sinful as me? I am a man full of pride and anger, yet the word I hear from the God who created me is "love."

When I was first saved back in 2006, I still had a lot of anger and pride. The more I read His word and the more people of God I surrounded myself with, I began to see a change concerning my outlook of life from all perspectives. *"This I recall to my mind; Therefore, I have hope. Through the Lord's mercies we are not consumed, Because His compassions fail not"* Lamentations 3:21-22 (NKJV).

We must seek forgiveness from those we have affected along the way. I remember when I realized the need to ask forgiveness for my anger. I went to every former player I could find and asked them to forgive me. Some looked at me like I was crazy, but others accepted my request. In the long run, those for whom you ask forgiveness will have a greater respect for you. They will respect the person you are today more than the person you once were. Some people are more ready to forgive than others. The deeper the hurt, the harder it is to forgive. The main lesson to remember is God will forgive our sin and will give us the freedom and clear conscience we need in order to move forward in our lives. People have no control over our freedom of guilt. If they choose not to forgive, then we must exercise our freedom to forgive them for their hard heartedness. I have found in time they will begin to see God working and change in our lives. We must have compassion for those who do not understand the power of forgiveness. We must pray for them.

Answer the Call

Once we implement the battle plan as listed in this chapter, the next step is the fun part. By now you realize that overcoming any spiritual stronghold will require effort. There will be days when we will not feel strong enough to resist the urge to sin. This is when our mighty God comes through for us. If it took us time to get here, it may take us time to get out. Some of you reading this book may claim victory within a reasonably short period of time, others may take longer. Either way, applying constant pressure on any stronghold will eventually allow it to succumb to the awesome power of a God who loves us and desires the very best for us.

Nothing is more powerful than God's love. Before I began my battle with sinful anger, I did not see God at work in my life. It took me almost two years before I was able to rid my mind of being constantly angry. Along the way I realized the journey was completely worth it. I faced moments of weakness. I felt the mighty hand of God at work in my life. Through much prayer and applying the steps as listed in this chapter, I began to experience victory.

I still struggle with anger, but today it feels different. I have much more control over my mind, and am able to give much more thought and consideration when needed. This is all because of God's power. One of my favorite stories in the Bible is when the Apostle Paul was struggling with what he called "a thorn in his side". Some biblical scholars believed he was referring to an issue with eyesight. Others believe he was dealing with a group of people called "Judaizers". These Judaizers were people who would follow behind Paul as he would preach the free gift of salvation. After Paul would leave the village, Judaizers would come in behind him stating his claim was only partially correct. They would go on to explain you also had to perform works in order to achieve salvation. In truth they were doing this in order to take money from the new Christians. The Apostle Paul pleaded with Jesus three times to remove this thorn in his side, but Jesus corrected him. The Apostle Paul writes

> *"And lest I should be exalted above measure by the abundance of revelations, a thorn in the flesh was given to me, a messenger of Satan to buffet me, lest I be exalted above measure. Concerning this thing I pleaded with the Lord three times that it might depart from me. And He said to me, 'My grace is sufficient for you, for My strength is made perfect in your weakness.' Therefore, most gladly*

I will rather boast in my infirmities, that the power of Christ may rest upon me. Therefore, I take pleasure in infirmities, in reproaches, in needs, in persecutions, in distresses, for Christ's sake. For when I am weak, then I am strong" 2 Corinthians 12:7-10 (NKJV).

We are all given a thorn in the flesh. Whatever our infirmities are, God allows them as a tool to teach us and to grow closer to Him. This "thorn in our side" is a reminder that God will walk through any obstacle with us. Imagine if mankind had no obstacles or hindrances. Human beings are lazy by nature. Yet humans are wired by God for success. When our sin nature gains control of our being, we often do not do what is right or healthy for our minds and bodies. We are always at our best when we have purpose. In order to have success, we must work at our craft. Our thorn may be a spiritual stronghold or an addiction. For others, this may be laziness or being a workaholic. All of these shortcomings are here to help us to become better people. It causes us to run to God when life seems out of line. When our car breaks down we call a mechanic. God is the mechanic for your soul.

How do we achieve freedom from a stronghold such as sinful anger? We answer the call. We cry out to God and start living in victory. This does not mean we won't have a slip up here and there. However the more we apply God's word, and the more we flush anger out of life, the more victory we achieve. God may leave a little bit behind that might require attention from time to time, but remember even school teachers and doctors need to take refresher courses in order to stay sharp at their craft.

All you can do to correct the past is to repent and seek forgiveness from God and man. God desires us to take our mess and turn it into a message. Like Apostle Paul, we should boast in our infirmities. Be happy to proclaim the mighty work God has done. Begin to set the example for future generations. Battling strongholds now leaves a legacy we can be proud to pass down. Remember, our greatest cheerleader is God Himself. *"The Lord is not slack concerning His promise, as some count slackness, but is long suffering towards us, not willing that any should perish but that all should come to repentance"* 2 Peter 3:9 (NKJV).

DISCUSSION

1) When is anger considered a sin?

_____

_____

_____

2) Do you believe your anger could be generational? Or a learned behavior? _____
Why?_____

_____

_____

_____

3) Do you believe Anger can sometimes be a good thing? _____
Why?_____

_____

_____

_____

4) Explain when anger was a good thing in your life._____

_____

_____

_____

5) What was Jesus' reason for getting angry? _____

_____

_____

_____

6) Have you sought out forgiveness from an offense you have caused to someone? Explain: _____

_____

_____

_____

7) What are your thoughts concerning God's love for you?

_____

_____

_____

_____

CHAPTER FIVE

Depression

Depressive disorder, otherwise known as Depression, is more than just a bad mood, feeling sad or going through a rough time. It is a mental health condition that requires understanding, possible medical care and intervention by a mighty God. What some professionals in the medical field fail to understand is depression may also be a spiritual stronghold. The U.S. National Library of Medicine reports more than 19 million teens and adults suffer from depression. Oftentimes with early detection, diagnosis and a personalized treatment plan, many people can get better. Yet no healing is complete without an intervention and a relationship with God

According to the National Alliance on Mental Illness, some people will only experience one depressive episode in a lifetime, but for most, depressive disorders recurs. Without proper treatment, episodes may last a few months or up to several years. At least seven percent of the American population has had at least one major depressive episode in the past year. People of all ages, racial and ethnic backgrounds suffer from depression.

Causes of Depression

Depression does not have a single cause. Physical illness, a life crisis or practically anything can bring on depression. Some of the causes may include:

Changes of the brain – Imaging studies have shown that the frontal lobe of the brain becomes less active when a person becomes depressed. Hormones in the body may also be a cause of depression. If someone's body doesn't produce the proper amount of serotonin, they will experience depression. This is similar to someone's body not producing enough insulin.

Drug abuse – According to NAMI, approximately 30% of those who suffer from depressive disorder suffer due to drug abuse.

Environmental – Where a person lives, or the surroundings associated with a certain lifestyle can contribute to depression.

Fear – Uncertainty and lack of hope could contribute to depression.

Genetics – Mood disorders can run in the family (Generational curse)

Life circumstances – Relationship changes, marital status, death and finances, etc. can bring on depressive episodes.

Medical conditions - People who have a history of suffering from ADHD (attention deficit hyperactivity disorder), anxiety, chronic pain, medical illness and even sleep deprivation can experience depression.

Medications – One of the side effects of some prescribed medications can be depression.

Physical Symptoms of Depression

- Changes in our appetite
- Lack of concentration
- Less activity
- Loss of energy
- Lack of interest
- Hopelessness
- Irritability
- Physical aches and pain

Having a depressive disorder can also contribute to suicidal thoughts.

Photo by Donna M. Courson

In order to confront and defeat depression we must build a strategic battle plan. Discovering where our depression comes from is our first step in defeating it.

There are certain cults in existence today who claim in the name of religion that only God is responsible for a healing of any kind and medication is not an option to getting well. Due to this irrational way of thinking, family members are denied medical care. While I do believe that they are correct in believing that God can heal any illness or disease if He so chooses. However I believe it is ludicrous to think of all of the knowledge and medicines God has created, that one would not be permitted use them for the expressed purpose of healing the mind or the body.

Legend has it there once was a man who knew of a great storm coming. All the while being aware of this storm, he made no attempts to prepare. His neighbors asked, "Are you not leaving in order to avoid the storm?"

"No," the man replied, "God will save me."

Eventually the storm came and brought flood waters into the man's home. A small paddle boat with rescuers paddled by the house."Do you need help?" asked the rescuers.

"No thanks," replied the man, "God will save me."

The waters rose, and the man was stranded on the roof of his house. A helicopter flew by and a voice came over a loudspeaker. "We're sending down a rope to save you!" "No thanks," yelled the man, "God will save me."

The man was swept away by the waters and drowned. In Heaven while speaking to Jesus he asked,"Why didn't you save me Lord?" Jesus replied, "I sent your neighbors, a boat and a helicopter. What more did you want me to do?"

It is unthinkable to not use every resource necessary to help us defeat depressive disorder. There are medications available, as well as many other types of treatment. It is equally as crazy to not reach out to the Great Physician to cure us from our mental illness. Many times we only treat the symptoms and not the actual disease. This is no different with depression. What about a renewing of the mind? To only focus on the medical side of treatment means our depression might once again rear its ugly head. The only permanent solution is using the resources available that can defeat the strongholds in our mind, and that is Jesus Christ. *"I have said these things to you, that in me you may have peace. In the world you will have tribulation. But take heart; I have overcome the world."* John 16:33 (NSV).

Is Depression a Sin?

Depression is a commonly discussed issue among Christians. Some declare depression to be a sin because it reveals a lack of faith. Yet many people who suffer from depression do so due to a chemical imbalance of the brain. This being the case we must understand depression is no more sin than being diabetic. We can fall into depression when someone dies. This is clearly not a sin. The Bible says, *"Blessed are those who mourn, for they will be comforted"* Matthew 5:4 (NKJV).

Depression becomes sin when it separates us from God and steals joy. When this happens, we are in spiritual danger. Seeing your doctor and seeking medication can help you in the case of dealing with a chemical imbalance or a medical condition. Prescribed medication can also help in the area of stress. In every circumstance concerning depression, God's word should always be prescribed.

Wrong Medication

If a doctor prescribes a medication and depression ensues, contact the doctor immediately. Everyone responds to medication differently. Sometimes a prescribed medication for one person is not a good idea for another person. I have ministered to men who are on prescribed antidepressants and they have told me that when they began taking the medicine, their doctor tried different types of medications as well as different dosages. One man who played a large role in leading me to Christ always seemed to be happy and in a good mood. However, I could always tell when he was not on his medication because he seemed to be irritable. He eventually shared with me it was because he was out of his antidepressants. Later I found the incredibly low dosage he was taking was all he needed.

When I was going through depression my doctor prescribed a medication for me. The medication not only removed the guilt I was feeling, but it made me dangerously apathetic. I quit this medication. After I learned the man who led me to Christ was taking a different type of antidepressant medication, I went to my doctor and talked to him about it. Although I tried this medication for some time, the medication did not have the same effect on me. I eventually quit taking this medication and started looking for healing through reading the word of God. I found the joy and peace I was seeking.

In my case I discovered I had two different types of depression. My depression came from genetics and stress. I was able to control my depression once I began my walk with Christ. One of my favorite books in the Bible is the book of Philippians. The book of Philippians is one of Apostle Paul's most encouraging letters.

In this letter, Paul teaches Christ's followers how to deal with hard times and provides examples from his own life experiences. Paul wrote this letter in 59 A.D. during a two year prison term in Rome. Paul was under the watch of the Praetorian guard. The Praetorian Guard was a highly respected group of men. Their service to Rome was only 16 years instead of the normal 25 years. They received triple pay, abundant bonuses and a generous retirement pay. The Praetorians were also used to torture and execute prisoners. During their 8 hour shifts, the Praetorian guard had no choice but to stand by and hear Paul preach the good news of Christ from morning until evening. These guards looked on as Paul would dictate letters to the Ephesians, Philippians, Colossians and Hebrew Christians. Hearing Paul's teachings, these elite guards were turning their lives to Christ. Even in the darkest circumstances God's word was spread throughout the Roman Empire as the Praetorian Guard had connections throughout Rome, as well as the Emperor's household which consisted of family members, servants, and slaves. Through Paul's efforts people everywhere began to accept Jesus as their Lord and Savior and began fearlessly speaking God's word.

One of the greatest statements ever made by the Apostle Paul was written during his time in prison,

> *"For to me, to live is Christ, and to die is gain. But if I live on in the flesh, this will mean fruit from my labor; yet what I shall choose I cannot tell. For I am hard pressed to depart and be with Christ, which is better. Nevertheless, to remain in the flesh is more needful for you"* Philippians 1:21-24 (NKJV).

Paul was a man just like us. He had moments of despair just like us. Instead of allowing sadness to consume his every thought, Paul chose to find his worth through Christ. He found the joy that only Christ could provide no matter what the circumstance.

Finding Joy in all Circumstances

Everybody wants to be happy. The word *happiness* evokes visions of Christmas morning and children unwrapping gifts. We make chasing happiness a life-long journey, going on expensive vacations, owning big houses, collecting things and searching for new experiences. But what happens when our health deteriorates, the toys rust and become boring and depression sets in? (Notice how I said "when" not "if.")

The contrast to happiness is joy. Joy runs deeper and stronger since it is the confident assurance of God's love at work in our lives. In the introduction of the book of Philippians found in the New King James version of my study Bible, it says, "Happiness depends on happenings. But joy depends on God's love".

Charles Swindol once said "Life is 10% what happens to you and 90% of how you react to it. And so it is with everyone...we are in charge of our attitudes." Imagine how our lives would change if we flushed out the sadness and began filling our heads with the Word of God? Imagine if we thought to ourselves, "Enough is enough. I am no longer going to allow this sadness to consume me any longer!" Even in the case where medication is needed, imagine if we still chose to attack depressive disorder medically and spiritually. The choice is yours. Your strategic battle plan begins now.

Confront the sin

As we discussed, it is very possible your battle with depression might not be sin. If this depression is keeping you from the joy of life then it is considered sinful. In either case, it is a stronghold and we must confront this stronghold.

In the case of a chemical imbalance in your brain - Seek medical attention. *"And the Lord, He is the one who goes before you. He will be with you, He will not leave you or forsake you; do not fear or be dismayed"* Deuteronomy 31:8 (NKJV).

If your depression is due to drug abuse, seek professional counseling and God's divine intervention. "*The righteous cry out, and the Lord hears, and delivers them out of all their troubles*" Psalm 34:17 (NKJV).

If depression is due to location or life style, remove yourself from that environment. We often will not make changes due to finances, but if this situation is causing your depression, then how can we not make a change?

> "*I waited patiently for the Lord; And He inclined to me, And heard my cry. He also brought me up out of a horrible pit, out of the miry clay, and set my feet upon a rock, And established my steps. He has put a new song in my mouth. Praise to our God; Many will see it and fear, And I will trust the Lord*" Psalm 40:1-3 (NKJV).

If your depression is due to fear, please also read Chapter Seven of this book. If you are fearful of someone, go to the police and seek protection or consider going to a safe house. You do not deserve to be afraid of anyone or anything. Perhaps professional counseling may be in order, as well. But don't forget, "*...Casting all your anxieties upon Him because He cares for you*" 1 Peter 5:7 (ESV).

If depression is coming from a generational curse or genetics, God can heal you. "*For the law of the Spirit of life in Christ Jesus has made me free from the law of sin and death*" Romans 8:2 (NKJV).

Our life circumstances are in constant flux, and this can impact our mood drastically. If this is causing depression, hang on. In the case of a death, the Bible is very clear on this subject and it is understandable to be depressed for a time. Regarding relationship changes, marital status, finances etc. "*For I am sure neither death nor life, nor angels nor rulers, nor things present nor anything else in all creation, will be able to separate us from the love of God in Christ Jesus*" Romans 8:38-39 (ESV).

If depression is caused by medical conditions such as ADHD, anxiety, chronic pain, medical illness etc. Seek medical and professional treatment.

"Beloved, do not be surprised at the fiery trial when it comes upon you to test you, as though something strange were happening to you. But rejoice insofar as you share Christ's sufferings, that you may also rejoice and be glad when His glory is revealed" 1 Peter 4:12-13 (ESV).

If depression is a result of medications, work with a doctor. See the doctor right away or get a second opinion. *"Fear not, for I am with you; be not dismayed, for I am your God; I will strengthen you, I will help you, I will uphold you with My righteous right hand"* Isaiah 41:10 (ESV).

Seek forgiveness

As discussed, suffering from depression may or may not be a sin depending on our circumstance. One thing is certain in that seeking forgiveness is our first step in finding joy. Regrettably in the case of the death of a loved one, some may unintentionally become consumed with depression and become lackadaisical in our approach to move on from this sadness. Although there is no exact time table for mourning, some Jewish customs indicate that mourning was allowed for up to one year. In the case of Moses, the people of Israel mourned the death of Moses for thirty days.

I have found when I began to understand the realness of heaven, it made my period of mourning death much less painful. When my father died in 1993, I was not walking in faith. To everybody who knew me there was no difference in my behavior, but to my wife and children there was a great deal of change.

I did not realize I was mad at God. Instead I took my pain out on my family through a series of vents of anger. I ended up in an affair that went on for three years. This was my way of lashing out on life for taking away the only man who ever really meant something to me. My reckless lifestyle brought embarrassment to my family and depression to my spirit. I lost the respect of my friends and team parents and was a let down to my players. Once I realized it was so bad, I felt that the only way I could give my family some semblance of life was to move them to another town where my actions were not common knowledge.

I remember that following year the local newspaper wrote a sports article regarding my success as a coach. This eventually led to my new town's local high school reaching out to me to help coach the girls' softball team. We were at a preseason tournament when the girls from my former team heard I was on another field coaching a new team. The minute their game was over, they left the field and ran over to where my current team was playing and waited by the dugout.

I walked out of my dugout and received many hugs and tears. As the embraces continued, I looked through the darkness of the night and could see many of their parents on the other field. Depression engulfed me as I knew many were never given an explanation as to why I left Jacksonville Beach. Many had believed I abandoned these former players. What they did not know was some members of the city of Jacksonville Beach had previously invited me to return to my former hometown to throw out the first pitch of the season opener to commemorate the city's first ever state championship, but other members of the league blocked the gesture because of the knowledge of my affair.

With their coach yelling for them to return to their own dugout to play another game, the girls would not leave or let me get back to my game without promising to come watch them play as soon as my game ended. I did as promised. I felt like Daniel walking into the lion's den. I could feel the staring and the anger from some of the parents. I understood their feelings, but this was one time I refused to let my former players down. I stood behind the back stop and cheered them on. As the game ended and the bleachers cleared, only one parent took the time to make a comment to me. He said, "I haven't seen these girls play this hard since you last coached them."

I have learned mourning is not always about losing a loved one through death. For a very long time I mourned over the sin I had committed against my family, my God and my team. Through this I learned about forgiveness. When those young ladies ran over to my dugout, they did not ask why I abruptly moved my family out of Jacksonville Beach. Instead they came seeking me in love. This is the same way Jesus comes to us when we have sinned. Unlike many non-believers think, Jesus does not come bringing wrath (although there will be a time and place for this to happen), but open arms and a desire to forgive.

"Say to them; 'As I live, says the Lord God, 'I have no pleasure in the death of the wicked, but that the wicked turn from his way and live. Turn, turn from your evil ways! For why should you die, O house of Israel?" (Ezekiel 33:11 NKJV).

When we seek forgiveness for depression we must first forgive ourselves. Suffering from depression steals our joy. We must understand this and take that step in the obedience of Christ knowing that He is just and willing to forgive. When I was saved and began to understand the power of forgiveness, I spent a great deal of time not only seeking out these girls, I also sought out others for whom I have offended or hurt in life. I reached out to as many parents of these former players as I could to seek forgiveness.

Forgiveness is More for Us

Seeking forgiveness is not always about the people we have offended. When our actions are blessed by God we receive a peace that only He can offer. There may be times when we seek forgiveness and the other party may not be receptive. Our responsibility is first and foremost to God. Only He has the power to condemn us for our actions. *"Judge not, and you shall not be judged. Condemn not, and you shall not be condemned. Forgive and you will be forgiven"* Luke 6:37 (NKJV). The action of seeking forgiveness gives us power to overcome and allows us to move forward in the healing process.

There may be times when we still feel guilty of our offense. Our conscience will not let go of the sin. This is either the evil one's attempt to keep us in depression or our own depression attempting to control us. *"Even if we feel guilty, God is greater than our feelings, and He knows everything"* 1 John 3:20 (NLT). When God forgives us, He does not want us to live in the bondage of guilt. Living with guilt after God forgives us is even more offensive to Him. *"He has removed our sins as far from us as the east is from the west"* Psalm 103:12 (NLT).

Answer the Call

Once we have confronted our depression, we must answer God's call. God has called us to victory. Focusing on God's plan for our lives is the most important step in overcoming depression. Our depression will try to talk us out of God's call and keep us in a state of sadness. There will always be obstacles in our lives, especially when we have decided that we must make positive changes. You can call it laziness, sadness, guilt, procrastination, but its real name is Satan. Satan throws these obstacles at us because he does not desire us to live in freedom or in victory. He knows once we obtain it, he will then lose whatever grip he has on us.

Purpose in Life

Contrary to what some may think, God did not create us to simply eat, sleep, breathe, pay taxes and die. The world thinks of God as some giant dictator sitting on a crystal throne staring down at us with His finger on the trigger. If we don't follow His rules we are destined for hell. This is not true. In order to understand the real meaning of life and why we are here, we must simply go to His word. In the first chapter we examined our sin nature and how sin entered the world. We also discuss in spite of our sin, God loved us so much that he sent His one and only Son to take our place on the cross and to pay the penalty of sin which is death.

"For God so loved the world, that He gave his only Son, that whosoever believes in Him should not perish but have eternal life. For God did not send His Son into the world to condemn the world, but in order that the world might be saved through Him" John 3:16-17 (ESV). This is a terrible strategy for a cosmic dictator.

Our purpose in life is not just to accept this great gift of eternal life. God also desires for us to live in the here and now. For those who are not firmly planted in faith and don't understand that a life with Jesus does not mean that one must live under His wrath and forbidden to have fun. Living submissively to Christ Jesus gives us more freedom than we can ever imagine. The greatest single question every human being asks today is "What is my purpose, and why am I here?"

"Everyone who is called by my name, whom I created for my glory, whom I formed and made" Isaiah 43:7 (ESV). We were created for God's glory. Imagine building a house from scratch. Think of the work that was put in, and once it is complete you can step back and marvel at its beauty. You're proud of your creation, and you want to show it off. This is how God sees us.

"And the Lord God formed man of the dust of the ground and breathed into his nostrils the breath of life; and he became a living being" Genesis 2:7 (NKJV). *"Then God saw everything He had made, and indeed it was very good"* Genesis 1:31 (NKJV). If we wouldn't build a house just to tear it down, why do we think God would? God desires the opportunity to love and cherish his creation. *"Or do you not know that your body is a temple of the Holy Spirit within you, whom you have from God? You are not your own, for you were bought with a price. So glorify God in your body"* 1 Corinthians 6:19-20 (ESV). That price was the shedding of Jesus blood for your sin.

We are God's most prized creation. We also know God hates sin. When sin enters our lives, God cannot take up residence within us. How would you feel if you spent all this time building a house that was intended for you and someone else moved in before you? Thanks to Adam, we are all born with original sin. Sin is very strong. It caters to our senses. It feels good. We cannot remove sin on our own. We need help from the Holy Spirit.

In order to make room for God we must evict the sin through the power of the Holy Spirit. God gives us a choice on how to live. God will not take up residence in us until we invite Him in.

Regarding Love

Like any good parent, God has made sacrifices for His children. After all we have done for our children, the worst thing they could do to us is to go against our will for their own lives. The greatest offense we could bring upon God as his children is to live in sin. Sin separates us from our Father and His perfect plan for our lives. The greatest joy we can have is to serve God and one another in love. After all He has done for us, why would God allow someone to live in His home and ignore His rules for eternity? I certainly would not allow someone to bring their filth and bad habits into my home around my children. Before you know it, their sin becomes a disease and pollutes everyone else in the home. Are we not children of God? Doesn't every good parent want to protect their children as best as they can?

When we follow the will of God and ask Him into our hearts, our reward is not just eternity, but also for the here and now. We are given wisdom, peace, joy and the knowledge that the evils of this world has no power over us. When there is the death of a loved one, we will still grieve, but not in the sense that our loved one is gone forever. We realize through God's grace this earth is nothing more than a part of our journey and more is yet to come. If one has accepted Christ, they will most assuredly see them again. This is the other part of why we are here on earth and why we exist, to help others understand the great gift of salvation and to be God's messengers of His good news which is called the Gospel.

Indeed, we were created for His glory. Here is what He says in His scripture regarding His desire for you:

> *"You did not choose Me, but I chose you and appointed you that you should go and bear fruit and that your fruit should abide, so that whatever you ask the Father in my name, He may give it to you"* John 15:16 (ESV). *"For we are His workmanship, created in Christ Jesus for good works, which God prepared beforehand, that we should walk in them"* Ephesians 2:10 (ESV).
>
> *"For I know the plans I have for you, declares the Lord, plans for welfare and not for evil, to give you a future and a hope"* Jeremiah 29:11 (ESV).

God wants you to live a joyful life and that is a life only He can provide. This does not mean you will not have obstacles along the way. When you are walking with God, every obstacle can be a learning tool which you can use to offer support or wisdom to someone else who is suffering from a similar situation. This is why Christians face tribulations and possibly why we suffer from depression. It can be a stronghold, or it can be used to help others. Now that you understand the reason why you are here, let's take the next step for implementing our battle plan!

Building boundaries in your life

Billy Graham once said, "I have never known a man who received Christ and ever regretted it." Having a personal relationship with our Lord and Savior is clearly the greatest step we can take in overcoming depression. As discussed in our previous chapters, the best way to flush out any stronghold in our lives is to fill our minds with the irresistible love of Christ. Read and meditate on His word. Understand our brain never rests. What kind of thoughts are we entertaining? Building boundaries around our thoughts is a great way to help with depression. When a depressing thought or a sadness enters our minds, we must fall back on that boundary as an impenetrable wall that will not allow negative thoughts to penetrate it. Negative thoughts often create negative reactions.

Keep a Journal

Make notes of the times in your life where you've witnessed God at work on your behalf. When depression attempts to enter your thoughts, take out the journal and read the stories from the past where God has been working. This is a great way to flush out the bad thoughts and replace them with the good thoughts.

Seek accountability

We must share our weaknesses with a trusted, Godly friend, and tell them when we feel at our lowest. This is a great way to have help staying in the Bible, keeping up with medications, doctor's recommendations, and other interventions in place to avoid depression. Remember even the strongest Christian can suffer from depressive disorder. No matter where we are in our journey, Christ is interested in healing all of us.

Seek God

Finally seek God. He is the one who can heal you if He so chooses. If He chooses not to heal you then I would suspect, He is leaving your depression within you as a "thorn in your side" (2 Corinthians 12:8-10). God will use this to help keep us grounded and constantly dependent on Him. He does this so He can use us to help others and to stay more self aware.

DISCUSSION

1) Do you suffer from depression?

   _____

   _____

2) How often does it occur?
   Once a week_____
   Once a month_____
   All of the time?_____

3) What type of depression do you believe you suffer from?_____

   _____

   _____

4) Do you believe your depression should be considered a sin?
   Yes_____ or No_____
   Why?_____

5) What do you believe your purpose in life is?

   _____

   _____

6) Is your depression preventing you from living the life God is calling you to have?
   Yes _____ No _____

7) Can you find joy in your life no matter what?_____
   Discussion:

   _____

   _____

8) Do you currently use a journal?
   Yes_____ No _____
   If no, do you intend to start using one?
   Yes _____No _____
   Why?_____

   _____

   _____

9) Who do you intend to use as your accountability partner? _____

   _____

   _____

CHAPTER SIX

Discipline

How can discipline be a spiritual stronghold? When used properly, discipline can be the greatest asset outside of God Himself. If we rely too much on our own self discipline or lack any whatsoever, then we are in danger of discipline becoming a stronghold in our lives.

What is discipline

According to the Merriam-Webster dictionary, Discipline is explained two different ways. 1) To punish or penalize for the sake of enforcing obedience and perfecting moral character. 2) To train or develop by instruction and exercise especially in self-control. In either case, discipline as explained by the Merriam-Webster dictionary is a good practice to use in life.

Lack of discipline

Not much can disrupt our lives like lacking discipline. Lack of discipline breeds character issues, laziness, illiteracy, physical health issues, as well as sin. The greatest secret hiding place evil can be found is within our mind right in between choice and reason. The seven deadly sins has a direct connection to a lack of discipline. The seven deadly sins are lust, gluttony, greed, sloth, wrath, envy, and pride. Let's look at what scripture says about these seven deadly sins.

<u>Lust</u> is an uncontrollable passion or longing, especially for sexual desires. *"Flee also youthful lusts; but pursue righteousness, faith, love peace with those who call on the Lord out of pure heart"* 2 Timothy 2:22 (NKJV).

<u>Gluttony</u> is an excessive ongoing consumption. This could be from food or drink. Gluttony is overindulgence, *"Do not mix with winebibbers, or with gluttonous eaters of meat; for the drunkard and the glutton will come to poverty, and drowsiness will clothe a man with rags"* Proverbs 23:20-21 (NKJV).

<u>Greed</u> can be an excessive pursuit or being over possessive of material things. This isn't always hoarding things, but rather never feeling like we have enough. *"Let your conduct be without covetousness; be content with such things as you have. For He Himself has said 'I will never leave you nor forsake you"* Hebrews 13:5 (NKJV).

<u>Sloth</u> is an excessive laziness or an act to not purposely utilize one's ability or talent. *"Go to the ant, you sluggard! Consider her ways and be wise, which having no captain, Overseer or ruler, provides her supplies in the summer, and gathers her food in the harvest"* Proverbs 6:6-8 (NKJV).

<u>Wrath</u> is an uncontrollable anger or hate for another person. *"Beloved, do not avenge yourselves, but rather give place to wrath; for it is written, 'Vengeance is Mine, I will repay,' says the Lord"* Romans 12:19 (NKJV).

<u>Envy</u> is the desire to have something belonging to someone else. *"Let us not become conceited, provoking one another, envying one another"* Galatians 5:26 (NKJV).

<u>Pride</u> is an excessive view of one's self. *"Thus, says the Lord: Let not the wise man glory in his wisdom, let not the mighty man glory in his might, nor let the rich man glory in his riches; But let him who glories glory in this, that he understands and knows Me,"* Jeremiah 9:23-24 (NKJV).

How often in our lives do we find a lack of discipline to be the main culprit to losing a job, contracting Type 2 Diabetes, or simply missing out on the important experiences in life? How often do we choose to miss church on a Sunday morning due to a late Saturday night? We seem to have no issue being a little sleep deprived if this were a golf outing, fishing trip or a tailgate. A lack of discipline can range anywhere from overeating, choosing a gluttonous life style, not setting the alarm clock and being tardy to work, to not putting in the proper quality family or quiet time. Satan gives little effort to someone who suffers from a lack of discipline because they are experts at self destruction. I speak more of myself than anyone I know. Let's just say if ice cream were a drug, I would be in the gutter begging for change. My love for cake and ice cream, as well as over-eating has been my downfall when it comes to my quality of life and waistline.

Don't Assume

There are instances where someone who may have an appearance of a lack of discipline may suffer from different types of physical or mental conditions, or perhaps is in a low season of life where finding a job evades them. It is not our job to assume, it is our job to walk alongside. *"Live in harmony with one another. Do not be proud, but willing to associate with people of low position. Do not be conceited"* Romans 12:16 (NIV).

For those of us who suffer from a lack of discipline, there is a very good chance we already know this condition is destroying our lives. There are scenarios where we may know someone who does not understand the ramifications from a lack of discipline or even perhaps a lack of knowledge. We have a responsibility to minister to that person in love and to help educate the individual of this stronghold. *"He will die for lack of discipline, and because of his great folly he is led astray"* Proverbs 5:23 (NLT).

When my wife Robyn and I were raising our daughters, we did not have a lot of income. We would purchase low cost meals for dinner which included a great deal of processed foods. We never had time to steam vegetables and roast meats because we both worked long hours in order to make ends meet. Little did we know that we were instilling bad eating habits in our children while poisoning all of our bodies. We would hear of eating healthy, but we had developed a taste for sweets and pasta. We assumed that eating healthy simply did not taste as good. Over time these poor habits caught up with me and as my discipline to exercise began to fade, I developed Type 2 Diabetes.

It wasn't until my oldest daughter Heather married Derek that things started to change. Derek has a passion to cook tremendous meals and loves family gatherings where he gets to provide home cooked meals. It was through Derek where I saw a different approach to healthy eating. I watched as Heather and Derek would raise their children and teach them the importance of proper eating. I watched my oldest granddaughter eat a piece of fruit as if it was a bowl of ice cream. My eyes were opened to my lack of discipline and to a new way of understanding food.

It was not until Derek joined our family did I began to see how my poor choices in diet played a major part in my health issues today. Being from the south, my grandmother, mother and aunts where fabulous when it came to preparing fried foods. I love fried chicken. I have also learned eating like this must be done in moderation. Was this a lack of discipline on my part, or was it simply a lack of knowledge? It would be easy to claim it was a lack of knowledge until Derek entered my life, but today I have no excuse for my poor eating habits other than a lack of discipline.

I have a friend who is a physical beast. At the age of 55 his discipline for proper eating and exercise has served him well. I watched him once be challenged by a young man at church who had a reputation for having great speed. As they were walking out of the men's ministry meeting, I watched my friend Derek in dress shoes race this high school teen at a moment's notice. As they raced, I watched Derek not only out run this speedster, but "talk trash" to him as he was crossing the finish line. The young man claimed he was caught off guard by Derek and challenged him to a second race. Derek obliged and on the second race beat him a second time all the while talking trash to him again as they crossed the finish line.

Everytime I think of my friend Derek, I am reminded that there was a certain time in my life when I could have put in the same work ethic at properly eating and exercising. Although I am not sure I could outrun a high school speedster at the age of 55, I would most certainly have enjoyed a healthier lifestyle which would also have an effect on my self-worth. The difference is where Derek put in the time to train and physically discipline himself, I did not. I chose cake and ice cream.

I understand that growing older is a part of life, but I have certainly done nothing to help myself turn back the clock of my youth. I am one of those who tends to put off diets until tomorrow. In truth, tomorrow never comes. Is this laziness? A bad habit? Or is this a spiritual stronghold? We can be considered lazy if this is a temporary condition, but if we are constantly putting off doing something that we know will improve our life, then there is a very strong chance we are dealing with a spiritual stronghold.

Where does a lack of discipline come from?

Generational – Some experts may argue as to whether having a lack of discipline can result from a generational curse. God speaks of the generational curse in the book of Exodus.

> *"The Lord, the Lord God, merciful and gracious, long suffering and abounding in goodness and truth, keeping mercy for thousands, forgiving iniquity and transgression and sin, by no means clearing the guilty, visiting the iniquity of the fathers upon the children and the children's children to the third and fourth generation"* Exodus 34:6-7 (NKJV).

The question may arise, "Can sin be passed down from one generation to another?" The answer is absolutely yes. I think we can all agree the seven deadly sins are connected to a lack of discipline. Any one of these seven conditions can be passed down from one generation to the next, but through the forgiveness of a merciful God, a generational curse can be removed.

> *"But what does it say 'The word is near you, in your mouth and in your heart' (that is the word of faith which we preach): that if you confess with your mouth the Lord Jesus and believe in your heart that God raised Him from the dead, you will be saved"* Romans 10:8-9 (NKJV).

Addictive Behavior –This type of addiction as discussed in Chapter Three is a disorder of the brain's reward system. Our brain can develop a craving for something such as sleep or sweets just to name a few. Have you ever exercised for the purpose of losing weight only to reward yourself when you lose a few pounds by eating a sweet? Many people do this. There are a wide range of genetic and environmental risk factors that can develop a lack of discipline.

Learned behavior – A lack of discipline can be learned from someone else. This was modeled to you when you were in the influential ages of your life. We can learn these behaviors from anyone who has been put in authority over us at different times in our lives.

Good Discipline over Lack of Discipline

Being disciplined can be very good when we practice the behavior as mentioned in the beginning of this chapter. The word discipline can be explained two different ways.

1) **To punish or penalize for the sake of enforcing obedience and perfecting moral character.** Without this type of discipline we would live in a world of chaos. Sometimes we must enact good discipline on our children. Our police and judicial system use corrective discipline for adults who choose to not live by the culturally accepted moral standards.

2) **To train or develop by instruction and exercise especially in self-control.** I have never met a person that ever thought being disciplined can be bad. There is always a level of respect for those who have the discipline to train their bodies to be physically fit or for people who discipline themselves for success whether it be in the world or the workplace. Those of us who resent others who demonstrate discipline are envious because it reminds us of our lack of discipline.

Photo by Kevin Carden

The Bible teaches us the positives of being disciplined.

> *"For God gave us not a spirit of fearfulness; but of power and of discipline."* 2 Timothy 1:7 ASV

> *"Whoever heeds discipline shows the way of life, but whoever ignores correction leads others astray."* Proverbs 10:17 ESV.

"Whoever loves discipline loves knowledge, but whoever hates correction is stupid." Proverbs 12:1 ESV.

"Rather, he must be hospitable, one who loves what is good, who is self-controlled, upright, holy and disciplined." Titus 1:8 ESV.

Too Much Discipline?

If we are to cover the issue of too much discipline as being a spiritual stronghold, we must acknowledge when discipline overload becomes an idol. I am not suggesting when you see a man who is muscle bound beyond the normal spectrum you should assume he is somehow over indulging or being over disciplined. There are times when issue of too much discipline can be a spiritual stronghold.

When we view our self-discipline as equal to God we have a problem. We should have nothing we regard in higher esteem than our almighty God. When we do this, it becomes our God. *"You shall not have no other gods before Me"* Exodus 20:3 (NKJV). A.W. Tozer once said, "What's closest to your heart is what you talk about, and if God is close to your heart, you'll talk about Him." When a thought or action consumes our very fiber, it becomes a spiritual stronghold.

To determine whether we are dealing with a spiritual stronghold of consuming discipline or a spiritual stronghold of having the lack of discipline is to ask ourselves what we think of most. For instance, if you worry about your job all of the time to where it consumes your every thought then your job has become your God and your spiritual stronghold. Anything that takes the place of God in our lives is sin.

When we see a bodybuilder with muscles on top of muscles that does not necessarily mean his training has become his God. He may just enjoy his craft of being a bodybuilder and excel in this area. If he wakes up on a Sunday morning and would rather go to the gym than church, he might have an issue with a spiritual stronghold.

There is only one area of over indulgence of discipline that is acceptable to God. This can be found in Luke 10:27 (NKJV), *"You shall love the Lord your God with all your heart, with all your soul, with all your strength, and with all of your mind, and your neighbor as yourself.*" To love anything else or anyone other than God that much is considered sin.

Confront the Sin

The first thing we must do is cry out to a just and forgiving God. He is the only one who can set us free from this bondage of a spiritual stronghold. "*For we do not wrestle against flesh and blood, but against principalities, against powers, against the rulers of the darkness of this age, against spiritual hosts of wickedness in heavenly places*" Ephesians 6:12 (NKJV).

Where we often fail is when we deceive ourselves into thinking we are strong enough to overcome any spiritual stronghold on our own. We sometimes think we can overcome spiritual strongholds with our own willpower. Pastor Zach Terry from First Baptist Church in Fernandina Beach once said "Willpower is like a muscle. Over time it will fatigue and that's why you must flee." God has promised to make a way of escape. Many times, the way of escape is to not even give the temptation a passing thought, but rather to turn and run from it. Call out to God through prayer and ask for His protection and strength. "*But you, O man of God, flee these things and pursue righteousness, Godliness, faith, love, patience, gentleness*" 1 Timothy 6:11 (NKJV). We must fill our thoughts with things of God and not with lusts, gluttony, greed, sloth, wrath, envy or pride.

Knowledge is power. Educate yourself on a ways to stay healthy physically, emotionally, and spiritually. Find an accountability partner who will help you break free from spiritual bondage. We must then begin to put into place good practice habits.

Practice Makes Permanent

We can't make anything perfect, but we can make permanent habits that will benefit us both spiritually and physically. Repetitive thoughts and muscle memory are essential to creating good discipline for the mind and body. Think of all the years that have been wasted practicing bad habits and thoughts. Lack of discipline is generated in the mind. Our brain adjusts our bodies to be receptive to these unhealthy choices, and eventually our bodies create a false need for bad foods, drugs etc, tricking us to believe our survival is dependent on these unhealthy practices.

The brain's reward system will cry out for more while all along destroying the body. Just like an alcoholic will feel the pull to a bar or an addict struggling to kick the addiction, the brain will attempt to trick you into feeling like it needs the very thing that is hurting you.

When I coached travel softball, we took a team to Orlando, Florida for a tournament. We continued through the winner's bracket which gave us a night of competition off. I decided to reward the girls by taking them to a restaurant that was well known for milk shakes. As each girl placed her order, I noticed my center fielder standing back and not participating in the milkshake feast. With great surprise this 16 year old, all-state caliber player shared that she had never had a milkshake. After getting her parents permission, I was honored to buy this athlete her first milkshake. I also felt terrible when she spent the rest of the evening with an upset stomach. Her body was trained to only eat healthy foods. Her athletic play and stamina throughout her young life was evidence of the good habits her parents had instilled in her.

In order to reverse a bad habit or an unhealthy lifestyle we must "re-train" our minds and bodies to do things the way God intended. This helps eliminate a lack of discipline. We can never forget we all are born with a sin nature. The mind and body will desire things that are not good for us. We must master our own bodies in order to eliminate what is not good for us.

> *"Or do you not know that your body is the temple of the Holy Spirit who is in you, whom you have from God, and you are not your own? For you were bought at a price; therefore, glorify God in your body and in your spirit, which are God's"* 1 Corinthians 6:19-20 (NKJV).

In order to break the chain of poor choices or bad habits we must ask God for intervention. I have found when people are able to confront the sin, seek forgiveness, and answer the call, amazing things can happen. They have been able to flee from poor life choices, fill their minds with thoughts of God and begin an incredible journey towards spiritual healing.

Sixty Day Battle Plan

In order to break the bondage of poor life choices regarding discipline, we have found the most effective way is by using the sixty-day battle plan. Sixty days may seem like a long time, but when you measure the years of unhealthy choices, I think we can all agree the effort required will be well worth the journey. On average it will take about two months before a new behavior will become a habit. I have found a combination of studying the word of God along with the sixty-day battle plan is an extremely powerful combination.

Remember God does not need a battle plan whatsoever. Can God instantly heal you? Yes. But God often prefers to go through the battle with you. But why? It builds character, self-confidence, obedience as well as an appreciation for His love. Through this journey of healing you have the opportunity to grow an up close and personal relationship with him.

How to prepare for your sixty day battle plan (Set goals)

If we don't have a personal relationship with Jesus none of this works. That means we are still trying to deal with our sin on our terms, and God doesn't bless that. Once the foundation is established we must set goals that will help us work through our journey of purging the spiritual stronghold. Here are seven steps you may consider.

1) Start small. – Most people want to create big change as quickly as possible. While some have been successful, most are not. This requires a tremendous amount of willpower. Remember your willpower is like a muscle and will fatigue. If you overwork a physical muscle you can cause more damage than strength. This is why I recommend small steps over the course of your sixty days.
2) Get hooked on your habit. – Educate yourself. Read articles that discuss the benefits of a good life change. Also read the book of Philippians.

3) Write down your battle plan. - Use a calendar with a start date to begin your sixty day journey. Don't forget to include prayer time.

4) Start a journal.- Write down goals and log in your success as well as your failures. Enjoy every victory no matter how small it feels. Tell your accountability partner about all of it.

5) Change your immediate environment. - Stop going to places that promote unhealthy choices. Get rid of the cookies. Never go to the supermarket hungry. Don't go to the bar. Don't go on your computer when you are alone. If you have friends who promote poor habits, share with them your desire to change. Ask them to honor your requests. If they refuse, get rid of them.

6) Surround yourself with others who will hold you accountable. Start a small group where each of you can talk about your victories and failures.

7) Incorporate prayer and personal Bible study time. When things get tough, pray and ask God for intervention.

Once you start your sixty day journey of healthy life choices, do not quit. If you quit, then you must start again. This sixty day plan is changing the dynamics of your mind, as well as your body. You must resist self in order to be successful.

Finding God

The one great benefit to working through this process is God will begin to reveal Himself in ways never thought possible. I have ministered to many men who have gone through this sixty day journey, and they've all said this experience has drawn them closer to God.

Practice makes Permanent

Have you ever been to a football game and watched as the teams are going through warmups before kicking off? You will see some very simple movements such as swim moves (defensive linemen making a swimming action with their arms), or practicing a run or pass pattern, yet a ball is never thrown to them. The purpose of these simple moves is for muscle memory and mind control. In the fast-paced action of a game the players will not have time to think of what type of move to use on the opposing player. Through muscle memory these moves become instinct.

These same practices should be applied when changing your body and mind concerning discipline. It's important to get into a routine of eating the right foods and making healthy lifestyle choices. You must fill your mind with the positive and flee from the negative. Train yourself to read God's word at the same time every day and do not let anything get in the way. Train your mind to desire the good things in life and master your mind to flee from the negative. While we won't reach perfection on this side of Heaven, we can make permanent lifestyle changes that can be part of our legacy.

Seek Forgiveness

Once we realize our shortcomings we must always seek forgiveness from our Savior. There are people in our lives we may have hurt along the way. Don't hesitate. Seek them out and ask them for forgiveness.

Often forgiveness is not so much for others as it is for honoring God with our actions. Those we've offended may not forgive us. With a loving heart and a desire to be forgiven from those we have offended, God will reward our actions with the freedom to move forward. This also means you must be willing to forgive those who may have offended you. *"For if you forgive men their trespasses, your heavenly Father will forgive you. But if you do not forgive men their trespasses, neither will your father forgive your trespasses"* Matthew 6:14-15 (NKJV).

Answer the call

We now have a battle plan of defeating both sides of the discipline stronghold. *"Don't put it off; do it now! Don't rest until you do"* Proverbs 6:4 (NLT). The sooner we begin this process, the sooner we can be healed. Our flesh will try to convince us to put it off another day, but chances are our flesh will find another excuse tomorrow. God knows this which is why He gave us Proverbs 6:4.

Our only chance of success is being obedient to His word. Once we are saved, no evil spirit can enter our bodies, but they will still attempt to whisper negative thoughts into our ears. It's almost like a dog whistle. Humans can't hear it, but the dog can! Our friends cannot hear the evil one speaking to us, but we can! We cannot allow these spirits to convince us that we are just lazy and never going to change. God has a very different plan for us!

DISCUSSION

1) Of the seven deadly sins, circle the ones you believe causes you the biggest problems? Lust – Gluttony – Greed – Sloth – Wrath – Envy – Pride

2) If you suffer from a lack of discipline, where do you believe this stronghold comes from? Generational____ Addictive behavior____ Learned Behavior____

3) What is your God? _____
   _____
   _____
   _____

4) How often do you pray? _____
   _____
   _____
   _____

5) Do you have an accountability partner? _____
   If so what is their name? _____
   If you do not have an accountability partner?
   Who do you intend to ask? _____

6) Will you use the sixty day battle plan? _____
   When will you start?
   Date: _____ Time:_____

7) Who do you intend to ask for forgiveness?
   _____

   Who do you intend to forgive?
   _____

Photo by Kevin Carden

CHAPTER SEVEN

Fear

Activebeat.com says "Fear is the most powerful emotion known to humankind. More powerful than love. Our very survival depends on it. Fear is triggered in the most primitive part of our brain. The part responsible for alerting us and protecting us from danger. Keeping us safe. Keeping us alive."

Six Most Common Fear Motivators

Fear of Failure – Nobody tries something in hopes of failing miserably. Regardless of what the movies say, failure is always an option. Fear of failure can be so paralyzing that it can rob our personal lives from quality time with our loved ones or keep us from achieving our goals because we won't take risks.

Fear of Success – For people who suffer from PTSD (Post Traumatic Stress Disorder), feelings associated with success can cause them to avoid excitement inducing circumstances because there is a preference for calm, control and safety. For many others, the idea of getting what they want is scary. What if it doesn't fulfill the need? What happens next?

Fear of dying – Having a persistent fear of one's own mortality can cause a person to crave safety and security above all else.

Fear of intimacy – Approximately 17% of the American population suffer from the fear of intimacy or a closeness in relationships.

Photo by Kevin Carden

Fear of Rejection – A fear of not fitting in or not being accepted into a new group. Many people who suffer from a low self-esteem suffer from a fear of being rejected.

Fear of Commitment – This is a combination of three of the above mentioned fears. People are fearful to commit to a relationship or a binding contract due to fear of rejection, intimacy, or failure.

This is not a complete list. There are also phobias, like a fear of spiders or flying. There is even a fear of fear. One of the most popular inauguration speeches in American history was in 1933 when President Franklin D. Roosevelt stated, "The only thing we have to fear is fear itself." No matter what type of fear we struggle with, we must look to see if it's a spiritual stronghold or just a natural reaction.

Where does fear come from?

We know fear does not come from God. 2 Timothy 1:7 says, *"For God has not given us a spirit of fear, but of power and of love and of a sound mind"* (NKJV). Did you know God encourages his followers to "fear not" 365 times in the Bible? That is a "fear not" for every day of the year!

Rick Warren said, "God did not intend for Christians to spend their days preoccupied with anxiety and worry." So where does fear come from? Let's examine the emotion of fear by looking at the keywords found in 2 Timothy 1:7.

The Spirit of Fear

There are some religions and cults which believe that there is a demonic spirit of fear that can enter our body and wreak havoc. However fear is a battle that occurs in our mind. If we are saved by grace, no demonic spirit can enter a body where the Holy Spirit already dwells. This does not mean we cannot have a demonic spirit whispering in our ear as an attempt to sway our thoughts. Pastor John MacArthur said, "Proponents of today's spiritual warfare movement say yes [that demons can inhabit a believer's body]. But the Bible makes it clear that such a claim has no justifiable basis. Nowhere do we see anyone rebuking, binding or casting out demons from a true believer. A clear implication can be found in 2 Corinthians 6, for example, is that the indwelling Holy Spirit could never have cohabitation with demons."

Fear can be something we are born with which falls into the category of the generational curse. Most of the time fear is an emotion that we have created. In this passage when Apostle Paul talks about the *spirit of fear*, he is talking about an emotion, a thought process, or a barrier, that we create within our own mind.

Hoarding is a bad habit so one could say that a person has a spirit of hoarding. Gluttony is a bad habit so some might say we have a gluttonous spirit. To better understand 2 Timothy 1:7, simply replace the word "spirit" with the word "habit." The English language is not sufficient enough to help us to better discern God's word regarding fear. Thankfully, God, in His omnipotence, gave us answers on how to defeat our fear regardless of where we might think it originates. Further study of 2 Timothy 1:7 states God gives power, love and a sound mind.

How can fear be stronger than love? That's because love is not an emotion. Love is a choice. We will discuss this further as we move along through this book.

Defeating Fear

Power

We have the power of choice. When we sin there is no entity within us that can overcome us or force us to sin. This is a decision we make on our own. God gave us this power when He created us in His image. *"See, I have set before you today life and good, death and evil"* Deuteronomy 30:15 (NKJV). God clearly gives us the choice to make our own decisions.

> *"But if your heart turns away so that you do not hear, and are drawn away, and worship other gods and serve them, I will announce to you today that you shall surely perish; you shall not prolong your days in the land which you cross over the Jordan to go and possess"* Deuteronomy 30: 17-18 (NKJV).

God states here what happens when we make the wrong choice. We will not always make the right choices, but God has given us the ability to choose and that, in itself, is power.

Love

Love is the second weapon against the spirit of fear. *"There is no fear in love; but perfect love casts out fear, because fear involves torment. But he who fears has not been made perfect in love. We love Him because He first loved us"* 1 John 4:18-19 (NKJV). Love is a choice.

"For I am persuaded that neither death nor life, nor angels nor principalities nor powers, nor things present nor things to come, nor height nor depth, nor any other created thing, shall be able to separate us from the love of our God which is in Christ Jesus our Lord" Romans 8:38-39 (NKJV). Who is perfect love? Jesus Christ. A great deterrent to the spirit of fear is to channel our focus away from what is consuming us and embrace the consuming love of our God.

Sound Mind

Our third weapon against the spirit of fear is a sound mind. How many times do we unnecessarily worry about something that never happens? Think of all the times over the years we have wasted on situations that never transpire! God has given us a sound mind, so we must use it.

> *"For the weapons of our warfare are not carnal but mighty in God for pulling down strongholds, casting down arguments of every high thing that exalts itself against the knowledge of God, bringing every thought into captivity to the obedience of Christ, and being ready to punish all disobedience when your obedience is fulfilled"* 2 Corinthians 10:4-6 (NKJV).

In 2 Timothy 1:7 the spirit of fear is destroyed. Having the power to choose, the love of God and a sound mind conquers fear so long as we are willing to make application of God's word to our lives. Fear is not an evil spirit. It is an emotion. Let's read this verse again *"For God has not given us a spirit of fear, but of power and of love and of a sound mind"* 2 Timothy 1:7 (NKJV). *"As His divine power has given to us all things that pertain to life and Godliness, through the knowledge of Him who called us by glory and virtue,"* 2 Peter 1:3 (NKJV).

God's word will overcome our fear every time. Pastor and author Max Lucado once stated, "Meet your fear with faith." Similarly Woodrow Kroll said, "The only antidote to fear is faith"

Why do we fear?

What is it today that cripples us from being the best father, husband and man we can be? Ever since the beginning of time man has gotten in his own way by placing limits on his ability. There are two types of men in this world: ones who tell themselves they can and those who tell themselves they can't. Henry Ford once said, "Whether you think you can, or you think you can't—you're right."

We are not alone in battling our fears. Everyone has a fear of something. Once we gain insight as to where this fear comes from, we have gained our first step in taking control of this crippling and life stealing thought process.

My former pastor Darryl Bellar has always said, "Let go and let God." What does this mean? We have to trust God in every area of our life. How often do we do this? How much time do we spend worrying about things we cannot control such as strongholds, losing a job, a failing marriage, a wayward child or being told we don't measure up. The Bible is very clear on this subject when Jesus said:

> *"Therefore I say to you, do not worry about your life, what you will eat or what you will drink; nor about your body, what you will put on. Is not life more than food or the body more than clothing? Look at the birds of the air, for they neither sow nor reap nor gather into barns; yet your heavenly Father feeds them. Are you not of more value than they? Which of you by worrying can add one cubit (hour), to his stature?"* Matthew 6:25-27 (NKJV).

When the spirit of fear arises God will give us the strength and wisdom to conquer it. When you are feeling fearful or afraid,

> *"Be anxious for nothing, but in everything by prayer and supplication, with thanksgiving, let your requests be known to God; and the peace of God which surpasses all understanding, will guard your hearts and minds through Christ Jesus"* Philippians 4:6-7 (NKJV).

Fear is simply what we make it out to be. When I used to coach sports, I would teach how fear can rob us from the best experiences in life. How often would we practice unmeasurable hours, honing our skills to be the very best athlete we can be, only to reach game time and our nervousness steals away what could have been a memory of a lifetime? I always taught that our greatest weapon was not our skills, but how we approach the game. No matter the circumstance no moment was ever too big for my players because they understood the real opponent was fear. Often my teams were less talented or not as big and strong as our opponents, but we won games because my players refused to let all of the work and sacrifice be robbed by fear.

My 1994 Jacksonville Beach girls' softball team won the Florida State Championship, the Southeast Regional Championship, and came within one run of winning the National Championship through work ethic and dedication. Through the understanding that fear was nothing more than an emotion which can be controlled, the game was never too big for them. These were twelve-year-old girls. If they can overcome the moment, then so can we.

Men Need Each Other

Many of us succumb to fear because we isolate ourselves within the four walls of our homes. We live our social lives through the internet. Men, in general, are terrible at reaching out to someone for help. We are raised to believe "boys don't cry", and that is a lie from hell. We isolate ourselves. We limit ourselves to calling someone a "friend" on social media which is very misleading. I have over 700 "friends" on social media, 50 of whom I may actually know. Do we know who their children are? Where they work? Men need each other. Imagine if men could simply open our hearts and be willing to be led by other Godly men of wisdom, to learn God's word and to apply it to ourselves and our families. This is what I have found in the Men's Ministry.

I believe every man desires to be a good father and a good husband. Sadly, many of us have no one to look to for guidance or did not have a good role model. The good news is it's NEVER too late for us. God is still on His throne and desires a personal relationship with us. There are Godly men who have started the ball rolling, redefining what a real man should be in our world. We only need to use our spiritual tool box (the Bible), and make the effort to seek out these wiser, smarter, men of God.

Origin of Fear

"But if God is the creator of everything, how is the spirit of fear not created by God?" Fear did not enter into existence until Adam and Eve committed the original sin against God. After eating the forbidden fruit,

> *"Then the eyes of both of them were opened, and they knew that they were naked; and sewed fig leaves together and made themselves coverings. And they heard the sound of the Lord God walking in the garden in the cool of the day, and Adam and his wife hid themselves from the presence of the Lord God among the trees of the garden. Then the Lord God called to Adam and said to him, 'Where are you?' So he said, 'I heard Your voice in the garden, and was afraid because I was naked; and I hid myself"* Genesis 3:7-10 (NKJV).

This is the first time fear is mentioned in the Bible. God gave each one of us the ability to make our own choices. Adam's emotions got the best of him because he knew he had sinned against God. This is also the first time human sin entered the world. Since man has the power of choice, we created the spirit of fear, not God. Our fears are a manifestation of sin. Adam was never afraid until he chose something other than God.

Unbearable Fear

What happens when we experience a catastrophic event or an unbearable fear is inflicted upon us? Circumstances in our lives can be life threatening and there is no time to prepare or apply a thought process to preparing or confronting our fears. At some point in our lives there may be a moment when a fear will arise that is beyond our control. I commit to you there will never be a day when God will not be present. This is why reading the word of God daily is such an important part of learning how to deal with our fears. Four times in the Bible God says, "I will never leave you or forsake you." *"Be strong and of good courage, nor be afraid of them; for the Lord your God, He is the One who goes with you. He will not leave you nor forsake you"* Deuteronomy 31:6 (NKJV). Suffering a fear that is greater than we can bear will always reveal the realness of God. "There are no atheists in foxholes" is an undeniable realization that even the most adamant non-believer will at some point cry out to an omnipotent God.

One of the most heart wrenching moments in the Bible was when Jesus was in the garden of Gethsemane.

> *"And He was withdrawn from them (disciples), about a stones throw, and He knelt down and prayed, saying, 'Father, if it is Your will, take this cup from Me; nevertheless not My will, but Yours, be done'. Then an angel appeared to Him from heaven, strengthening Him. And being in agony, He prayed more earnestly. Then His sweat became like great drops of blood falling down to the ground"* Luke 22:41-44 (NKJV).

Was Jesus trying to get out of His mission? Absolutely not. Jesus exposed His dread of the coming trials, but He also reaffirmed His commitment to do what God wanted. The cup He spoke of meant that he was aware of the terrible agony He knew he would endure in order to die for the sins of the world. This was indeed a moment in history when unbearable fear gripped our Savior. In spite of His fear, Jesus took on the sin of the world on our behalf. His fear proved Jesus was a man, but on the third day He proved He was God.

It was during this time Jesus taught us that in our flesh we are nothing, but with God, all things are possible. God the Father did not take the cup away from Jesus because God loves us that much. Jesus second moment of fear came when God had to turn His back on Him just as Jesus took on the sin of the world while hanging on the cross in your place and mine.

> *"Now from the sixth hour until the ninth hour there was darkness over all of the land. And about the ninth hour Jesus cried out with a loud voice, saying, 'Eli, Eli, lama sabachthani?' that is, 'My God, My God, why have You forsaken Me?"* Matthew 27:45-46 (NKJV).

Jesus was not questioning God. He was quoting the first line in Psalm 22 as a deep expression of the anguish He felt when He took on the sins of the world. For the first and only time in history, Jesus was separated from His Father. This was what Jesus dreaded

as He prayed to God in the garden to take the cup from Him. The physical agony was horrible, but even worse was the period of spiritual separation from God. Jesus suffered this double death so that we would never have to experience eternal separation from God.

Fear is a stronghold and God has given us the power, love and a sound mind to defeat it. Jesus paid the sin debt once and for all. Jesus agonized over the pain and the moment of spiritual separation from the Father on our behalf. Jesus, although fully God and fully man, feared the moment at hand, but confronted fear at its very core and defeated death.

> *"Seeing then that we have a High Priest who passed through the heavens, Jesus the Son of God, let us hold fast our confession. For we do not have a High Priest who cannot sympathize with our weakness, but was in all points tempted as we are, yet without sin. Let us therefore come boldly to the throne of grace, that we may obtain mercy and find grace to help in time of need"* Hebrews 4:14-16 (NKJV).

Confronting our fears

There is one way we would have to deal with the same anguish of fear as our Jesus did. That is when we reject the very Salvation Jesus is offering and died for. The cup, as mentioned by Jesus in Luke 22, is our sin nature and all the sins we have committed and will commit. There can be nothing as painful or as scary than being separated from a just and Holy God. God does not desire that anyone should go to hell. This is the very reason He allowed Jesus to die on the cross for you and for me. *"The Lord is not slack concerning His promise, as some count slackness, but is longsuffering toward us, not willing that any should perish but that all should come to repentance"* 2 Peter 3:9 (NKJV).

Fear is a stronghold. Fear will keep you from enjoying the good things in life. Jesus desires for you to have no fear, but to have joy and to have it more abundantly. *"The thief does not come except to steal, and to kill, and to destroy. I have come that they may have life, and that they may have it more abundantly."* John 10:10 NKJV. The thief that is mentioned in this verse could very well be your fears.

Confront the sin

In order to defeat the stronghold of fear we must confront this emotion head on. God is willing to set us free from this bondage, we just have to ask. Unlike addictions, depression or pride, fear affects all of us. Every person on this planet will experience fear and will experience it often. *"Cast all your anxiety on Him because He cares for you"* 1 Peter 5:7 (NIV). Fear never entered the world until Adam fell. Fear has always been a choice. Remember, God tells us 365 times in the Bible "fear not." God desires that we confront this sin because He knows the freedom we can experience through trusting Him. Nobody wants to live in fear. Fear is a part of our sin nature, but God is our salvation and He did not give us the spirit of fear. Therefore we must confront this sin and address it with God by seeking forgiveness for allowing fear to consume us. Ask for His power to confront the sin.

Seek Forgiveness

I sometimes don't think we understand how much God desires to have a personal relationship with us. God loves to hear from us. This is why having a strong prayer life is so important in our walk with Jesus. Some might ask "if God knows everything, then why do we need to pray?" When having a conversation with our children, don't we know what they are going to ask? Yet, we wait to hear our children ask because of our fondness and love for them. Is not God our Father? *"And when you pray, do not keep on babbling like pagans, for they think they will be heard because of their many words. Do not be like them, for your Father knows what you need before you ask Him"* Matthew 6:7-8 (NIV). God does not want you to come to Him with some magnificent, fictitious prayer. Prayer is talking with God. He already knows what we are feeling even when we are mad at Him. He can take it! Seek forgiveness for being afraid, and then make a greater effort to honor His word.

Answer the call

Once we have confronted our sin and sought forgiveness, we now have a responsibility to proclaim the victory as given to us from Jesus our Lord. Jesus desires that we share our stories so that others might be influenced by His love. We push forward with power, love and a strong mind.

With God, all things are possible

My wife, Robyn, has dealt with many battles in her life. Her father was diagnosed with cancer when she was 12 years old. Her fifteen-year-old brother, Brett, had no choice but to quit junior high school and take over the family business so that they could make ends meet. Brett was not yet old enough to drive, so their mother would drive him to service calls. Frequent car trips out of town for her dad's cancer treatments and surgeries caused him to be gone on weekdays and return on weekends. Robyn was often alone. She had developed several issues, fear of bridges, claustrophobia, anxiety and a fear of flying.

She was naturally shy. All of this coupled with being married to a self-absorbed, proud man who had many anger issues left Robyn with few opportunities to live life to the fullest. In October of 2013, Robyn developed several imbalance issues and was tested and diagnosed with a permanent condition.

Many years earlier Robyn traveled with me to Michigan to make sales calls. On the flight to Michigan, Robyn's fear of flying had become very evident. As the week ended and we were returning to the airport to fly home, Robyn became physically sick and began to cry out begging me to not put her on another plane. We had no choice but to rent a car and drive the one-thousand-mile trek in one weekend back to Florida, so I could be back at work on Monday. When our daughter, and her family moved to California it was very devastating for Robyn as she knew there would be no way for her to fly out to visit our family.

In March of 2018 while traveling to a women's Bible study, Robyn was broadsided by another vehicle. Her car spun, rolled and was flipped upside down. Her doors were wedged shut by the impact and she was left hanging upside down in the car with only the seat belt supporting her. Immediately while the vehicle was flipping, a sudden calm came over her! As she was trying to process what was happening, she felt a presence in the car with her. Suddenly a man who was never identified somehow slipped through a back door of the car. She asked him to pray with her. He began speaking words of encouragement and telling her that she was going to be okay. She never got to see his face since all airbags had deployed and covered the windows. He stopped once more after getting out and said, "You are going to be alright." The paramedics arrived and had to break the windshield in order to get her out of the vehicle. The paramedics placed her on backboard loaded her in the ambulance and took her to the hospital. I tried desperately to find this guy for weeks to no avail. We did hear the man's name was Eric, but as heroes often do, he performed this act of love expecting nothing in return and no desire to be recognized.

Robyn was taken by ambulance to the hospital only to be released with minor bruises. A few days later Robyn began to ask me about my thoughts on Eric. "Was he an Angel?" she asked. I asked why she made such a comment? She then shared with me ever since the accident she believed she had been delivered from her fears. In April, I decided to book a flight for May to see my daughter, Heather, for Mother's day. As I was booking the flight, Robyn became upset with me. She then said the words I never thought I would hear, "But I want to go, too."

She believed God used the accident to heal her from her fears. I booked the tickets and we flew to the John Wayne Airport together for the first time. You should have seen the look on our families faces when Robyn walked out of the terminal. Shocked by her surprise arrival, everyone was in tears. Not only did Robyn enjoy the flight, she wanted the window seat on the way home. She answered the call.

> *"And we know that in all things God works for the good of those who love Him, who have been called according to His purpose."* Romans 8:28 NIV.

Robyn flying for the first time in 18 years (May 12, 2018)

1) What do you fear? _____
_____
_____

2) Why do you fear? _____
_____
_____

3) What does power, love and a sound mind mean to you?
_____
_____

4) Where does fear come from?
_____

Explain:_____
_____
_____

5) What does it mean for you to "Let go, and let God" _____
_____
_____

6) Have you ever experienced a moment when a fear was greater than you could bare? _____
Explain:_____
_____
_____

7) In what way has this chapter on fear helped you? _____
_____
_____
_____

8) When is the last time you had a really good conversation with God? _____

_____

_____

_____

CHAPTER EIGHT

Jealousy

Jealousy is "an unhappy or angry feeling of wanting to have what someone else has; an unhappy or angry feeling caused by the belief that someone you love (such as your husband or wife) likes or is liked by someone else" (Merriam-Webster.com).

That's all of us, isn't it? Everyone at some point has dealt with jealousy in either matter. There are many forms of jealousy. Dictionary. com explains jealousy this way, "Jealous, resentment against a rival, a person enjoying success or advantage itself. A mental uneasiness from suspicion or fear of rivalry. Vigilance in maintaining or guarding something." Ever have a girlfriend? Then you've been jealous. Ever felt unhappy because you wished you had a car like your friend has? There it is again.

Jealousy has caused more fights, passion and outright wars than any other emotion known to man. Even God Himself has expressed jealousy in His word. Man has a basic instinct to want to be the center of attention. As children we want the toy another is playing with even if another toy just like it is available. Why? Fear causes the child to feel lonely. Insecurity makes us feel like we are not good enough. It results in the need for competition. A persistent feeling of jealousy can damage relationships, especially when our jealousy is irrational. Jealousy contains a wide range of emotions and behaviors.

Insecurity

Insecurity is an uncertainty or an anxiety about oneself and a lack of confidence. Men may suffer from this much more than women do. Our reasons may vary from an over obsessive parent to an event that may have destroyed our confidence. Here's an example. If somebody took a puppy and placed him in a dark closet, the puppy will be fearful of the dark closet and have no way of escape no matter how loud the animal cried out. Once that puppy grew into a large dog and allowed out of the closet, the dog would learn that it never wanted to go back into the closet again. He might even resort to violence if needed.

This can also have an opposite effect. Instead of the puppy growing into a dog who will retaliate against its fear of a dark closet, the puppy could grow into a dog who is constantly afraid and never fight back. This also happens in people. We develop certain anxieties for things we cannot understand. We tend to run away or block out experiences so as not to interrupt the little world we have created for ourselves. Dealing with anxiety is a very real situation. Our heart begins to race, we feel a shortness of breath and, in some cases, we might feel as if we are having a heart attack.

Being insecure has frequently cheated us from the many good things in life. When we are in a relationship for instance, the moment we see our girlfriend or wife smile or interact with the opposite sex, we become jealous. We could build barriers between us and our significant other where they might feel they need to hide their interactions with others so as not to suffer our wrath. Situations like these cause the relationship to suffer, builds walls and eventually destroy the relationship.

We can get jealous at somebody else's success. We know we deserved that award, that promotion, that opportunity, and we get angry when we do not get recognized. Often we might even become upset with the person who was awarded, even though it was our insecurities that caused us to shield ourselves from the opportunity. We live in our own self-made prison, but remain jealous of others because of their success. We fail to realize our jealousies are of our own making because we lack confidence in ourselves and never take initiative.

Fear

To better understand fear and the effect it has on our lives, go back and review Chapter Seven. We sometimes find ourselves envious of others who do not suffer from the same fears in which we suffer. We want to be like them because all we can see are the things they have that we don't. We are afraid that somebody else is getting our blessings so we become jealous of them.

Competition

I have trouble finding fault with being competitive because a great majority of the time it brings out the very best in us. There are instances where jealousy does not play a factor in competition. Often when striving for personal achievement, we are being competitive against ourselves, pushing ourselves beyond our limits in order to become the best we can be.

Being jealous of someone who is better at something can be dangerous. Do we hold resentment towards them simply because they are more talented or perhaps, they may have put in the extra hours of work towards their craft? If we do, then jealousy is not good for us. When we give our all in any type of competition, and come up short, accepting defeat is a necessary lesson that we must learn. It teaches good sportsmanship and builds character.

I have no problem giving an award for an achievement, but kids today are receiving awards for simply getting up on a Saturday morning, getting dressed in their soccer uniform and showing up. This is wrong. What about the children who try harder or are more talented. They receive the same trophy. Weren't trophies created to award the victorious competitor? This type of thinking is creating a race of misinformed, lazy people. The problem is when a child grows into adulthood, they must learn that not everyone gets the same job. Often the person who works harder gets the job or promotion. We are now faced with a generation of a self-indulgent "have it your way," selfish and depressed people. I am worried that this upcoming generation who doesn't know how to win or lose will be overcome with the stronghold of jealousy.

No matter how sheltered we keep our children from the world, competition will one day rear its ugly head. We must teach our children to understand that we will win and lose in this world. When the losses come, we are to accept defeat with honor and live to fight another day. It is not an option to go into a jealous rage.

Two kinds of jealousy

As we mentioned in Chapter Four, there are two different types of anger. As with anger, jealousy can also be a good thing. Bible.org explains it best when discussing the two different jealousies.

"The marital relationship may be the best way to help us understand the difference between sinful jealousy and righteous jealousy. We can be jealous over our wife in a wrong way and a right way. For example, if we feel resentment or anger merely because our wife is talking to another man, that would be self-centered possessiveness and unreasonable domination – in other words, sinful jealousy. It would stem from our own selfishness or insecurity rather from our commitment to her and to what is right. But, on the other hand, if we see some man actually trying to alienate our wife's affections and seduce her, then we have reason to be righteously jealous. God gave her to you to be your wife. Her body is yours just as your body is hers. You have exclusive rights to enjoy her fully, and for someone else to assume that right would be a violation of God's holy standards."

God calls Himself a jealous God. To appreciate God's jealousy we first need to properly understand it. His jealousy is the kind that zealously protects a love-relationship which avenges it when broken. When God tells us that He is jealous, He means that He demands from those whom He loves absolute loyalty. He will vindicate His claim by stern action when betrayed. God is jealous of us because He loves us.

A better way to understand God's jealousy is to replace the word "jealous" with "zealous". Zealous means to show zeal or being devoted to a purpose, being fervent or enthusiastic. God loves us so much that he is zealous for us. *"For you shall worship no other god, for the Lord whose name is Jealous, is a jealous God"* Exodus 34:14 (NKJV).

(Notice the capital G? The word "God" means we are speaking of the almighty omnipotent God of Abraham, Isaac and Jacob. When we see a lowercase "g" means we are speaking of a false god. Many interpretations of the Bible miss this important fact.)

Is Jealousy a Sin

We mentioned there is a sinful jealousy, as well as a righteous jealousy. For many men today, jealousy has become a stronghold. Whether it be from our insecurity, our lack of confidence or a misguided competition, jealousy can be a tool in which the evils of this world will use against us. We can cause our own demise through jealousy.

Confront the sin

What are we jealous of? Is our jealousy causing us distress, hardship, loss of sleep or simply making life harder on us? There are times when the person we are in a relationship with gains some sort satisfaction when we are jealous of them. They will do things to make us jealous. However in more cases than not, our jealousy is of our own making. How different would our lives be if we could rid ourselves of sinful jealousy? *"A sound heart is life to the body, but envy is rottenness to the bones"* Proverbs 14:30 (NKJV).

Everyone will at some point deal with jealousy. How we respond to jealousy can be the difference to having peace in our lives to having turmoil. Once we discern our jealousy, we must ask ourselves, are we dealing with a righteous jealousy or a sinful jealousy.

Righteous Jealousy

In the case of righteous jealousy, we can obtain freedom by confronting the situation in love. If someone is causing you righteous jealousy, such as a man desiring attention from your wife, it is important that you confront this individual in a loving manner. I suggest you pray to God and ask for wisdom before confronting anyone who may be causing you to feel righteous jealousy. *"Do not be overcome by evil but overcome evil with good"* Romans 12:21 (NKJV). It is equally important for you to confront your wife and alert her to what the other man is attempting to do. Do not approach her in anger.

"Anger is cruel and fury overwhelming, but who can stand before jealousy?" Proverbs 27:4 (NKJV). If you approach either person and their response is negative, approach them again according to God's word.

> *"Moreover, if your brother sins against you, go and tell him his fault between you and him alone. If he hears you, you have gained your brother, but if he will not hear; take with you one or two more, that by the mouth of two or three witnesses every word may be established"* Matthew 18:15-16 (NKJV).

Sinful Jealousy

Sinful jealousy is a stronghold caused by your insecurity, fear or a misguided competition. Either type of jealousy can cause you pain. The key here is to immediately address the situation in love. How we respond to this emotion and the help we seek will determine the outcome. Confronting the sin is our first step in not only obedience to God, but also obtaining victory.

We must ask ourselves, is our jealousy merely a passing thought? Is our jealousy a bad habit that inhibits our quest for a joyful life? Is our jealousy consuming our every thought? We must turn to God's word for the answer on how to overcome this emotion:

> *"So, flee youthful passions and pursue righteousness, faith, love, and peace, along with those who call on the Lord from a pure heart"* 2 Timothy 2:22 (ESV).

> *"But as for you, O man of God, flee these things. Pursue righteousness, Godliness, faith, love, steadfastness, gentleness. Fight the good fight of the faith. Take hold of the eternal life to which you were called and about which you made the good confession in the presence of many witnesses"* 1 Timothy 6:11-12 (ESV).

Flee means to turn and run away. Do not entertain the thought but flee. Reach up to God and pray for His strength. Remember a stronghold is a battle of the mind. We have a choice in what controls us. If someone or something has the power to offend us, it has the power to control us. God does not desire for us to be controlled by anything, but rather to walk in His peace and His light. "*Take delight in the Lord, and He will give you the desires of your heart*" Psalm 37:4 (NKJV).

Using your Spiritual Toolbox

My biggest prayer is that throughout the reading of this book, people will realize how the Bible (our spiritual toolbox) contains every answer. The problem starts when we do not apply the knowledge we gain through God's word. Without God, we are nothing. How many times do we hear people say "I do not feel the presence of God?" The reality is God hasn't gone anywhere. It is man who walked away from God. God says four times in His word "I will never leave you or forsake you." Deuteronomy 31:8, Hebrews 13:5, Joshua 1:5, 1 Chronicles 28:20. ESV.

Seek forgiveness

Once we have confronted the sin, we must seek forgiveness. Not only from God but also from ourselves and anyone we have offended with the mishandling of our jealousy. God is the only one who can grant salvation, but God requires us to seek forgiveness from those we have offended. "*Bearing with one another, and forgiving one another, if anyone has a complaint against another; even as Christ forgave you, so you also must do*" Colossians 3:13 (NKJV).

When we seek forgiveness we must do so with caution. Are we looking for a free pass or to right a wrong? God knows our heart. I have seen instances where someone would seek forgiveness, but didn't feel any remorse. There is nothing worse than approaching someone apologetically, but our body language reflects a different attitude. God desires that we genuinely seek forgiveness with sincerity and humility. "*Therefore, confess your sins to one another and pray for one another, that you may be healed. The prayer of a righteous person has great power as it is working*" James 5:16 (ESV).

Forgiving Ourselves

We must understand that once we have repented and seek God, we must let go of our pain. If we don't learn to let go, we are then offending God all over again.

"If we confess our sins, He is faithful and just to forgive us our sins and to cleanse us from all unrighteousness" 1 John 1:9 (ESV). When we ask our Father for forgiveness, scripture says He is just to forgive. When we continue to carry that burden, are we not exhibiting a lack of trust in God's promise? *"If they fall away, to renew them again for themselves the Son of God and put Him to an open shame"* Hebrews 6:6 (NKJV).

We must realize once God forgives our sin, it is finished. So, we must be cautious to not mock Him or His gift of peace. When we do not forgive ourselves, all we are doing is giving power back to the stronghold in which God has already purged from our minds. You can read more about this subject in Chapter Ten.

Answer the call

With every step of forgiveness God requires a step of obedience on our part. One of the reasons God has not devoured this earth and burned us to a cinder is because there are people who don't know Him yet. We have a responsibility to share our personal experience with God so that others may realize His love. This is done by answering the call to share the good news of Jesus Christ. This book contains the absolute most heart- wrenching moments in my life. I would prefer that no one know about my sin, especially those in my family, but I understand that people on earth are dying and allowing Hell's doors to open because we as Christians sit by and do nothing.

I am convinced that absolutely no one desires to simply die and become worm food, or die and burn in Hell for eternity. There is a Hell, and those who do not accept Jesus as Lord over their lives will suffer eternal separation from a just and loving God.

We can answer the call by being an open book to those we know. We can share our testimony and our changed life. We do not have to live under the bondage of the stronghold of jealousy. God will give us the strength to overcome this mind-crippling emotion, but we must respond by answering the call.

Did you know the two most powerful actions in the universe outside of God Himself is prayer and forgiveness? So why are we not using these two actions to our advantage? Create your battle plan, confront your sin, seek forgiveness, answer the call, and drench every action with prayer.

DISCUSSION

1) What are some insecurities in your life? _____
   _____
   _____
   _____

2) Do you sometimes feel jealous over something due to your fears?
   Yes / No_____
   Explain_____
   _____
   _____
   _____

3) Have you ever experienced jealousy due to a feeling of misguided
   competition?
   Yes/No _____
   Explain_____
   _____
   _____
   _____

4) Have you ever experienced righteous jealousy?_____
   Yes / No_____
   Explain _____
   _____
   _____
   _____

5) How often do you use your spiritual toolbox?
   once per day?_____
   once per week?_____
   once per month?_____
   Never?_____

6) How often do you feel the presence of God in your life?
   All of the time_____
   Sometimes?_____
   Never?_____

7) Do you believe experiencing the presence of God could have something to do with how often you open your spiritual toolbox? Yes/No_____

Explain_____

_____

_____

_____

Leading Your Family

One of my mentors, Pastor Van Power, told a story of a 6th grade elementary school teacher who began an assignment by asking her class to finish the statement "I wish." She thought her students would say, "I wish I could have a new video game," or "I wish I could have a new bike," but what she got shocked her. Instead most of her students responded, "I wish my parents wouldn't fight." "I wish my daddy would come back home." "I wish my mom would pay as much attention to me as she does her boyfriend." "I wish I could do better in school, so my daddy would be proud of me."

"Leading your family" doesn't sound like a spiritual stronghold, but I've found over the years that the family is Satan's favorite place to attack! Many men have been left out in the cold when it comes to knowing how to be a father. Our fathers raised us the best they knew how, but many of us have been left without a solid, biblical view of fatherhood.

According to the U.S. Census Bureau, 24 million children in America – one out of three – live without their biological father in the home. Research shows when a child is raised in a father-absent home, the child is 47.6 % more likely to live in poverty. The risk of being mistreated also increases. A child being raised in a fatherless home is more likely to deal with drugs, to have behavioral problems and go to prison.

Want more? The fatherless.wordpress.com reported:

- 63% of youth suicides are from a fatherless home. (US Dept. of Health/Census)
- 90% of all homeless and runaway children are from a fatherless home.
- 85% of all children who show behavior disorders come from a fatherless home.
- 80% of rapists with anger problems came from a fatherless home.
- 71% of all high school dropouts came from a fatherless home.
- 75% of all adolescent patients in chemical abuse centers come from a fatherless home.
- 85% of all youths in prison came from a fatherless home.

This qualifies as a crisis.

On the other side of the spectrum, father involvement shows a higher likelihood of a child getting better grades in school. Daughters with involved fathers are less likely to engage in risky sexual behavior. Father involvement results in less stress for children. Men with whom I have a great deal of respect are the men who step up to the plate and raise a family even though they are not the biological father.

The biblical model of manhood and fatherhood is under attack in our culture. Simply turn on your television and watch the many programs who portray a dad as a mindless dolt who is the brunt of all of the jokes. Men today are working longer hours and working on personal hobbies rather than spending quality family time. We counter stress by running off to the golf range or to our favorite fishing hole leaving mothers to teach our sons how to be men.

There are many great women out there who are doing a tremendous job leading a single parent home, but I think we could all agree having an involved father would make life less stressful for the mother. The father brings a certain set of qualities and traits to a family that a mother does not possess and vise versa. What a sad state of affairs it is when the mother is forced to choose to live as a single parent so as to protect her children from fathers who can't, or won't step up. With no real male role model in the home, a boy's idea of manhood will come from wherever they can find it.

Headship in the Home

What is a real man? What is a good role model? What is the biblical image of being the Headship of the home? I once heard someone say, "No one ever made a rule book on how to be a man." I disagree. The Holy Bible contains every tool we need to be the man God is calling us to be and Jesus Christ is a perfect example for us to follow. We're not going to find the answer to this question in a world that can't make up its mind on what a man should be. Being headship of the home does not require perfection, but it does require investment and involvement. Some of the best fathers I know are men who make mistakes from time to time, but the family will follow someone whose focus is building a biblical family.

Being a headship of the home does not mean we rule with an iron fist, but rather through perseverance and love. Generational curses can be decimated when a man realizes his faults, lays them at the throne of Christ and places his family in God's hands. Reading God's word gives us wisdom in this. Where our fathers may have failed we will not. Maybe our parents did a great job at raising us and we simply did not pay attention, but it's never too late to restart.

Being headship of our home requires humility and follow through. Being the headship of the home does not require vast biblical knowledge, but just enough to be a step ahead of your children. If they ask a question that we can't answer, we have to tell them we don't know, find out the answer, and then follow up with them. What a great counter cultural example for our families!

Children see everything and they will grow up to mimic what they see. That's why allowing your children to see us praying and having family Bible time is of the utmost importance. To best explain the image of headship in the home is to simply open and use the spiritual toolbox. The image of being headship of the home is found through the power of love.

> *"Love suffers long and is kind; love does not envy; love does not parade itself, is not puffed up; does not behave rudely, does not seek its own, is not provoked, thinks no*

evil; does not rejoice in iniquity, but rejoices in the truth; bears all things, believes all things, hopes all things, endures all things" 1 Corinthians 13:4-7 (NKJV).

Raising children is not women's work. Before the Industrial Revolution took the man out of the home, child rearing and educating was a team sport. God made fathers and mothers complimentary. God created men and women in His image and our families function best when the two are working together. Make no mistake here, fathers will be responsible before God for how we take care of the family. This is the responsibility of being headship of the home.

Mother Teresa was once asked how we can best promote peace in the world and she said, "Go home and love your family." The way we fix the moral decay of our communities is by starting in the home. Every movement, every shift in society has begun with one person. Every man can make a difference in his own home.

The prevailing take away from Adam and Eve in the book of Genesis is the shame on mankind when Eve ate the forbidden fruit. What we fail to notice is Adam was right there with her all along. Adam watched her take the bite and when she handed him the fruit, he took a bite as well. *"So, when the woman saw that the tree was good for food, that it was pleasant to the eyes, and a tree to make one wise, she took of its fruit and ate, She also gave to her husband with her, and he ate"* Genesis 3:6 (NKJV). Today man continues to stand ideally by and do nothing as our families and community continues to slip away. This is called "living in the shadow of the first Adam". Through the teachings of Jesus (the last Adam), we can reverse this mind set. *"And so it is written, 'The first man Adam became a living being.' The last Adam became a life giving spirit."* 1 Corinthians 15:45.

Our world continues to fall further away from God, but the downward spiral does not have to be this way. In the book of Jonah, God had stated He would destroy the city of Nineveh, but when the Ninevites heard of their fate, they repented, and God spared the city. *"When God saw what they did and how they turned from their evil ways, He relented and did not bring on them the destruction He had threatened"* Jonah 3:10 (NIV). God kept His word in that He would one day destroy Nineveh, but it wasn't until some 150 years later. God also has a standing offer to us as found in 2 Chronicles 7:14 which says, *"If My people, which are called by My name, shall humble themselves, and pray, and seek My face, and turn from their wicked ways, then I will hear from heaven, and forgive their sin, and heal their land."* NKJV. The alarming thought about this verse is that God is not speaking to the lost. He is speaking to the saved. That's us. If we could only repent and serve God as He requires He would spare our land.

So What Happened?

The movie "Gone with the Wind" was released in 1939. Producer David O. Selznick had to pay a $ 5,000 fine for violating the Motion Picture Production code for using profanity. This was in the final scene of the movie when Rhett Butler said, "Frankly my dear, I don't give a d _ _ _." Today we can't go to an average movie without hearing the word G.D.. Satan uses time as a tool. He pushes the envelope slowly and methodically and we never see it coming until often it is too late.

So, what happened to the family? A little over one hundred years ago before our nation was known for industry, farming was a way of life. A typical family would raise an average of seven children because the children would play a role in running the farm. They would watch as dad would teach them the family business and the value of hard work. They would work alongside their father until it was dinner time in which they would then share a meal together huddled around the dinner table. They would talk about their day. Often after dinner and before bedtime, mother would read the Bible to the family.

Then came the Industrial Revolution. Many young men left the farm life hoping for a steady paycheck in the big city. Supporting a larger family became financially unreasonable forcing the family dynamic from seven children to two children per household. As the Christian family and morals dwindled, false gods, religions and a twisted way of thinking began to infiltrate the American way of life.

During the early twentieth century many men left their homes to defend our country and mom became the spiritual and moral supporter of the home. With the lack of men in the church, pastors began to change their sermons and tailored them more towards the issues moms would face daily. Eventually the wars ended and dads returned home to find Mom held down the fort admirably. Dad found himself feeling no longer needed and being left out of the decision making. He'd been gone a few years and missed out on the influential years of a child's life.

He buried himself in his work and believed his greatest worth to the family is to pay the bills and put food on the table. He came home from a long day's work exhausted, and the last thing he wanted to do was hear how mom's day went or go outside and play catch with the children. Mom was left holding the bag as Dad is finding his worth and value at his job. He bonded with his co-workers who were dealing with the same thing. The slow fade of the American family continued as Satan separated and infiltrated.

The 1940's and 1950's rolled by like a freight train. In the 1960's, Americans were involved in many kinds of cultural and political movements, which included the movement of women's rights. Enter the 1970's and the "Me decade." Today, we average 338 friends on social media, but in reality we only know nine friends. Only two of those friends are considered confidantes. Our families have stopped paying attention to the older generation because our lives are simply too busy. Our senior citizens end up alone and investing too much of their time with their poodles and cocker spaniels rather than passing down the many years of knowledge and wisdom to their family.

These factors have made men not knowing how to Biblically lead their families as a spiritual stronghold. Children today are growing up with little influence from a Godly man. Instead they have fathers who aren't engaged physically, spiritually, or emotionally. The lack of a father's role in the family today can be summed up in Harry Chapin's timeless song "Cats in the Cradle."

And the cat's in the cradle and the silver spoon
Little boy blue and the man in the moon
When you comin' home, dad?
I don't know when
But we'll get together then son
You know we'll have a good time then.

Not the real Jesus

The real kick in the jeans is when dad attends church with his family only to hear the preacher talk about a fair skinned, blonde haired, blue eyed Jesus that sounds better suited for a hand soap commercial than the Warrior and a King as described in the book of Revelation. The idea of a meek Jesus does not fit the role model dad has been searching for. So as the father finds more manly things to do on Sundays, church attendance dwindles, and Satan's methodical approach continues.

Jesus is a man's man. Hollywood and the church have done a poor job portraying the real Jesus. Jesus' earthly father was a carpenter, meaning Jesus most likely followed his earthly father's craft. Jesus labored with His hands for about twenty years before His ministry began. Jesus got his hands dirty.

> *"And when the Sabbath had come, He began to teach in the synagogue. And many hearing Him were astonished, saying, 'Where did this Man get these things? And what wisdom is this which is given to Him, that such mighty works are performed by His hands! Is this not the carpenter, the Son of Mary, and brother of James, Joses, Judas, and Simon? Are not His sisters with us?' So they were offended at Him"* Mark 6:2-3 (NKJV).

This was all a part of God's plan. The Messiah, unlike the prophet Samuel and John the Baptist, did not grow up in a priestly household where He could have devoted His days to prayer and the study of scripture while having access to the temple precincts. He also was not raised within a Pharisee's household like the Apostle Paul. Jesus was sovereignly assigned to ordinary people.

Jesus did not become God and then begin His ministry. Jesus was God at the beginning of the world. Jesus was God as He laid in the manger as an infant. Jesus was God on the cross and on the third day. Jesus is still God today. The people were offended by Him because they believed people had to be trained by an institution in order to possess this kind of knowledge. Jesus was the Son of God, but in the purest sense Jesus was like you and me. Due to His humble upbringing, Jesus never had a problem walking in the lowest parts of the town. This was where many people who needed a Savior lived. One of the most amazing qualities about Jesus is that He can get on any level and talk with us while still being a living example of how to live a life pleasing to God.

The purest sense of Jesus' power can be seen in Revelation 19:11-16 NKJV.

> *"Now I saw heaven opened, and behold, a white horse. And He who sat on him was called Faithful and True, and in righteousness He judges and makes war. His eyes were like a flame of fire, and on His head were many crowns. He had a name written that no one knew except Himself. He was clothed with a robe dipped in blood, and His name is called The Word of God. And the armies in heaven, clothed in fine linen, white and clean, followed Him on white horses. Now out of His mouth goes a sharp sword, that with it He should strike the nations. And He Himself will rule them with a rod of iron. He Himself treads the winepress of the fierceness and the wrath of Almighty God. And He has on His robe and on His thigh a name written: KING of KINGS and LORD of LORDS..."*

There is no question who this scripture is referring to. The fact that on Jesus' head were many crowns means He is the King of every nation. Jesus is called "The Word of God" in John 1:1. "Now out of His mouth goes a sharp sword, that He should strike the nations", *"For the word of God is alive and active. Sharper than any double-edged sword, it penetrates even dividing soul and spirit, joints and marrow; it judges the thoughts and attitudes of the heart"* Hebrews 4:12 (NIV). Does this sound like a weak Jesus to you? This is the same Jesus who took on the sin of the world, hung and bled on a cross on our behalf.

We allow our children to grow up wanting to be like Iron Man or Superman, but the real superhero is Jesus Christ. He is a living breathing example of an authentic man. He is a perfect image of what the head of the household represents. It's not too late. We can destroy the spiritual stronghold that is keeping us from being the father our children deserve and the husband our wives need. We can take back our families from the moral decay that is ripping our nation apart and we can save our community simply by becoming the man God is calling us to be.

Confront the Sin

Jesus is cheering for you at this very moment. Satan is going nuts right now because he knows he is absolutely no match for Jesus. As we discussed in the first chapter, the war between Jesus and Satan is over,, and Jesus is victorious. The only battle that can occur is when we buy into the lies Satan constantly manufactured since he met with Adam and Eve in the garden. Think of all the years Satan has spent slowly and methodically destroying families.We are on the verge of ripping our families away from his evil clutch. All he can do is whisper intrigues of sin in our ears. He cannot physically touch the saved or enter their bodies because they are occupied by that of the Holy Spirit.

> *"Be sober, be vigilant; because your adversary the devil walks about like a roaring lion, seeking whom he may devour. Resist him, steadfast in the faith, knowing that the same sufferings are experienced by your brotherhood in the world. But may the God of grace, who called us to His eternal glory by Christ Jesus, after you have suffered awhile, perfect, establish, strengthen, and settle you. To Him be the glory and the dominion forever and ever. Amen"* 1 Peter 5:8-11 (NKJV).

Begin the battle plan with a prayer. Ask God for direction. Be part of a Christian church who has a strong men's ministry, or help start a men's ministry of three or more men who want to fellowship. A church men's group who only meets once a month for breakfast is not a men's group, it's a social club. To lead a group does not require a charismatic leader who is a biblical scholar. There are plenty of resources to use.

I created the Christian Men's Association of North Florida (CMAN) to promote men's groups in local churches. Regrettably, many churches do not understand how to teach the biblical role of the man in the home. Some of the men do attend churches where men's ministry is simply not a concern for their church. CMAN meets once per month in hopes that other men will be convicted to meet as their own church group at least twice a month. When CMAN started there were only two men's groups in our community. While writing this chapter, I am happy to report ten different churches in our community have realized the need for men's ministry. That number is growing. So, we as a para-church ministry offer studies such as "33 The Series", "From This Day Forward" by Craig Groeschel, and "False Love" by Brad Hambrick from the Summit Church in North Carolina.

In 2003, the Baptist Press reported if the child is the first in the household to become a Christian, there is a 3.5% probability the family will follow? If the mother is the first to become a Christian, there is a 17% chance the household will follow. If the father is first, there is a 93% chance the family will follow. If a pastor wants to increase church attendance, they should go after the man! These numbers further prove God's design for the family. Like Voddie Baucham said, "Win the man, and the family will follow."

Being the head of the household is something God Himself has created men to do. This is not a man barking instructions to the wife and child with a "my way or the highway" attitude. This is clearly not the image Jesus portrays or talks about when He said, "...'Anyone who wants to be first must be the very last, and servant to all" Mark 9:35 (NIV).

The Apostle Paul told men, "Husbands, love your wives, just as Christ also loved the church and gave Himself for her. That He might sanctify and cleanse her with the washing of water by the word" Ephesians 5:25-26 (NKJV). When we begin to follow Jesus, we begin to understand the qualities needed to be the headship of the home has already been imprinted within our minds. In this fallen world, we are unable to cultivate the tools required to be a leader within the home. The more we focus on God with a desire to be Godly men, the more His image of headship within the home is revealed.

What we also need to understand is the women we are married to are also God's daughters. Just as we are naturally protective of our daughters, God is also protective of His daughters. With true headship comes great responsibility. Jesus died for His bride (the church), are we willing to die for our wives? My wife and I have always seen things differently. When she was hot, I was cold. When she wanted pizza, I wanted a hamburger. This was a problem in our lives for a long time, until I began to understand that I was married to God's daughter. I began working on this problem. I realized that it was not me who found Robyn and chose her to be my wife, but rather God chose her. Sometimes we don't realize our wives are a gift from God. Sometimes we give up too quickly on a marriage before it has time to be cultivated. Just as man is wired to be the headship of the home, the woman is wired to be submissive to the husband. "*Wives, submit to your husband, as to the Lord. For the husband is head of the wife, as also Christ is head of the church; and He is the Savior of the body. Therefore, just as the church is subject to Christ, so let the wives be to their own husbands in everything*" Ephesians 5:22-24 (NKJV).

The problem arises when men try to rule their home based on worldly views. The solution comes when a man begins to tap into God's design for marriage, rather than his own or the world's. God's word reveals a true reflection of headship. I believe with all my heart when a woman sees honesty and integrity in a man, they are naturally drawn to him. One of the most important needs for a woman is to feel safe and wanted. She also wants to be able to trust. When the man shows an inability to offer any of these, there will be complications.

A great book that helped us both understand the difference between a man and a woman is "Love & Respect", by Doctor Emerson Eggerichs. This taught me that our differences did not mean we were not compatible, but rather God purposely designed us with different strengths and weaknesses. As Robyn and I read through "Love and Respect", I began to see her differently and to appreciate our differences. It got to the point where we noticed how we complimented each other in different areas of our lives even after twenty years of marriage. I realized just how bad of a husband I was for most of our marriage. One of the key points of the book was to learn how to forgive each other as Christ forgave us. We begin to see our arguments for what they truly were, we learned how to choose a higher road and admit our weaknesses, and to apologize.

The Non-Christian spouse

Being the headship of our homes is hard when we have an unsaved wife. That is why the Bible implores us in 2 Corinthians 6:14 *"Do not be yoked together with unbelievers. For what do righteousness and wickedness have in common? Or what fellowship can light have with darkness."* NKJV.

But what happens when we are unevenly yoked to someone who is not a Christian? What happens if you get saved and your spouse does not know Christ, or we ignore the scripture as found in 2 Corinthians 6:14?

God says *"Likewise, wives, be subject to your own husbands, so that even if some do not obey the word, they may be won without a word by the conduct of their wives"* 1 Peter 3:1 (ESV). What this scripture is saying is the Christian spouse is to be a living example of Christ to the non-Christian spouse. When we follow God's design and we are submissive ourselves to God, and work to be the man God is calling us to be, our wives will take notice.

After I was saved in 2006 my wife had a hard time believing me. I had lied to her so often in my pre-Jesus era. I had proven myself to be untrustworthy. Robyn would listen to me, but she did not attend church with me because there was no trust in the home. We also know that when someone gets saved, they don't automatically become this spiritual superman who no longer has issues with sin. It's a process. Although I was saved and making progress, I still had issues with foul language and anger.

Robyn would not trust me. She eventually started going to church with me because I was bothered and felt that she was not supporting me. When I finally realized I might very well be on this spiritual journey alone, I began to earnestly pray to God to change my wife's heart. On December 1, 2007, I received a call from Robyn. She had been a non- practicing Christian all of her life. When the Holy Spirit got a hold of her, she had a heart change and began to trust me.

Confront the Sin

Not loving our families enough to lead them in Christ is sin. Love is a choice, not an emotion. We must love our wives and children, not out of duty, but out of desire. Perform acts of kindness for your family. Invite God into every situation including your intimate times in the bedroom. My friend, Chuck Lynch, told me anytime he and his wife get in an argument they would stop what they are doing, pull up a chair and get knee to knee together, then pray with one another. It's hard to carry on an argument when you're talking to God.

When we are wrong we must be quick to admit it, and when we are wronged we must be quick to forgive. Under no circumstances should we bring it up later. Our children shouldn't hear us degrade our wives. One day they will grow up and will remember your wisdom, as well as discern who is at fault on their own. When confronting sin, call it out into the open. Honor the scripture:

> *"Two are better than one, because they have a good reward for their labor. For if they fall, one will lift up his companion. But woe to him who is alone when he falls, For he has no one to help him up. Again, if two lie down together, they will keep warm; But how can one be warm alone? Though one may be overpowered by another, two can withstand him. And a threefold cord is not quickly broken"* Ecclesiastes 4:9-12 (NKJV).

I could write an entire chapter on this verse. As we nurture our relationships with Christ and our wives, this verse will begin to reveal itself on its own. The "threefold cord", as mentioned in this verse, is husband, wife, and God throughout eternity.

Seek Forgiveness

When I confronted my sin of not leading my family, I immediately addressed my issues with God. I asked Him to forgive me and to give me the wisdom and discernment to change my life, as well as, make a positive impact on my family.

I sat down with my wife. I explained to her that I understood what I had done to her. I explained to her I understood the ramifications of my sin. I told her I was willing to walk through the process of forgiveness with her, and she could take as long as she wanted. Divorce would no longer be an option because I was willing to prove my life change. I also made her aware that I was going to place God first in my life and in the center of our marriage. I asked her for forgiveness. I told her I was going to earn my position as headship of the home by setting the example and unconditional love towards her.

Photo by Kevin Carden

I then sat down with my children. I explained to them that I realized my sin. I admitted I was a terrible father and was going to work to learn how to be someone they would one day be proud to call dad. I asked them for forgiveness. I told them that their needs would come before mine. I explained to them that I would never be perfect, but I would point them to the One who is. I asked them to be patient with me as I learned how to do the right thing while on this new journey. I told them I was going to earn my position as their father by setting the example and unconditional love.

I then made my sin public to whoever would listen because I wanted them to understand my heart change. I wanted those close to me to hold me accountable. I went to every former athlete whom I coached and shared the story of my heart change. I asked them to forgive me. I asked my employees and boss for forgiveness.

I had no idea the power of forgiveness. Most forgave me. Some friends thought it was a joke, but through a changed heart they began to see the new me. I had to drench my issues in prayer. I fell often, but my wife, children and, most importantly, God were worth getting back up off the ground to fight another day. I lost friends along the way, but God has replaced them with a group of men for whom I hold dear.

For Divorced Men

In the article "Marriage & Divorce", The American Psychological Association reported the divorce rate in America is up to 50%. Sadly, this statistic is not much different in the church. I have been blessed over this past decade to have been able to minister to many men. Two of the most often discussed topics are sex and divorce. When discussing divorce, I have discovered regardless of fault, divorce causes a deep pain. In fact, the deeper I dug into the pain, the more I discovered a sense of failure, as well as an inability to forgive one's self. I believe a small part of this has to do with the way some Christian circles deal with the issue of divorce.

Yes, divorce is a sin. Nonetheless it is not a greater sin than any other. Just like any sin we commit in our lives, God is just to forgive. The Bible says when we earnestly seek forgiveness with a desire to walk in His love, God not only forgives our sin, He actually forgets our sin. *"For I will be merciful to their unrighteousness and their sins and their lawless deeds I will remember no more"* Hebrews 8:12 (NKJV).

This is impossible without the shedding of Jesus' blood at Calvary. Psalm 103:12 says God forgives our sin as far as the east is from the west. If He forgets our sin will His heart become broken every time we fall into sin? I have dealt with men who are sometimes unwilling to forgive themselves for divorce. As we discussed in Chapter Eight, we offend God when He is willing to forgive our sins and we continue to hold on to what God has forgiven. Divorce is mentioned 11 times in the Bible. Forgiveness is mentioned over 105 times in the Bible. Men who have experienced divorce need to understand the love of a forgiving

God. They must move forward with their lives. When we earnestly seek and ask God, He will forgive us. He may even allow a new love into our lives. If He does, love her according to God's design and not your own.

Answer the Call

Return the love back to God by sharing your story with others. Share with them how God can make things right again. When dealing with our spouses, children, friends, and coworkers, be a blessing to them. No one can argue with your personal testimony.

Five Elements of a Blessing

There are five different ways we can be a blessing to our family every day.

- A Word - Always be willing to offer a compliment to a child or a spouse. Encouragement is a great way to build confidence. Everybody enjoys positive reinforcement. Nurturing positive vibes throughout the home will lessen thoughts of negativity and get them to seek your advice more often.
- A Touch – It's one thing to compliment a spouse or a child, but when we include the compliment with a warm embrace or gently holding their hand, this makes the compliments personal and carries a greater degree of affection.
- A Value - The greatest value you can give a loved one is your time. Often we men will come home tired from work and the woman wants to talk about her day. Men listen to the tribulations of her day and attempt to offer advice and fix problems. Many times, she already knows how to fix the problem, she just wants to talk. Stop trying to fix her issues (unless she asks for your advice), and simply look into her eyes and listen.
- A Future – Planning a future together builds a sense of security. It's always a good idea when planning vacations or family outings to encourage input from your family. Always do things that will allow your family to see you intend to spend

the rest of your life with them and your sincerity in building a future together.

- Commitment – Be committed to your family. Always place their needs ahead of your own. Don't just tell them you are committed, show them. Watch the excitement on your child's face when she has a ball game which you were unable to attend, but you cancel your appointment and attend the ballgame instead. These are just a few small ways to express your commitment to your family.

Leading our families is a journey and not a race. Performing random acts of kindness, expressing love and appreciation towards the wife and children will build the home into an amazing fortress. It's okay to make mistakes along the way, as long as we are transparent with our families. In every scenario of failure, they need to see us go to God for guidance. One day we will not be around, and our children will become adults and have their own families. My prayer is we will learn how to demonstrate our relationship with God during difficult times so that they may follow our example after we are gone.

As families continue to dwindle it is important to understand the dynamic of our church family. Our children will move away and one day we may find ourselves much older and alone. I promise that having a church family can fill those times of loneliness and keep us active and engaged with life. Building great memories with our children (regardless of their age) will keep them wanting to come home as often as they can. Everybody loves a safe place. Now answer the call.

1) What are your thoughts regarding the statement "Satan separates and infiltrates?"

_____

_____

_____

_____

2) Have you seen this to be the case in your own personal life? _____

3) Describe a situation where this has happened to you?

_____

_____

_____

_____

4) Have you ever considered the fact that your significant other is also God's daughter? _____

How does this make you feel about her now? _____

_____

_____

_____

5) In what ways do you believe this chapter has helped you?

_____

_____

_____

_____

6) What are your thoughts regarding the comment "Love is a choice" _____

_____

_____

_____

7) How do you see yourself as being a Godly man? _____

_____

_____

_____

_____

8) What areas do you need to improve? _____

_____

_____

_____

_____

9) Has the ability to Lead your family according to God's will been a stronghold for you? _____

_____

_____

_____

_____

10) What must you do to change? _____

_____

_____

_____

_____

CHAPTER TEN

Letting Go

Of every stronghold mentioned in this book, none can be more damaging to your health and wellbeing than the inability to let things go. As I was writing I knew there must be a chapter addressing the stronghold of unforgiveness. As I reminisce on the men I have ministered to, not only during my Christian walk, but during my pre-Jesus era, I have found the inability of letting go pops up in a variety of ways. Not being able to let go is deadly. Some of us have never dealt with an addiction, lust, or pride, but every single one of us has dealt with not being able to let go.

I named this chapter "Letting go" because unforgiveness is only part of it. Sometimes being able to let go could also mean cutting out a bad habit or bad influence, like an unhealthy relationship. Maybe it's a job change so that we can see our full potential. Maybe our past is still holding us down. You must let go of situations that are keeping you up at night. *"Peace I leave you; My peace I give you. I do not give to you as the world gives. Do not let your hearts be troubled and do not be afraid"* John 14:27 (NIV).

Our battle plan throughout this book is to first confront the sin, seek forgiveness and finally to answer the call. "Letting go" is not about seeking forgiveness from others or forgiving ourselves, but allowing ourselves to forgive others.

Where does this stronghold come from?

If an injustice moves us to action against it, then it can be a good thing. If it inspires us to be better people, then it doesn't control us. However, when holding on to something from our past keeps us from an action, it becomes a stronghold.

Unforgiveness comes from two places: Our sin nature and Satan. These two evils are nothing more than a thief, keeping us from enjoying the peace God has promised us. *"The thief comes only to steal and kill and destroy; I have come that they may have life and have it to the full"* John 10:10 (NIV). Our sin nature fuels the inability to let go of a hurt or an anger. Then there is Satan who is quite fine with us having the inability to forgive because all he has to do is stand by and watch us destroy ourselves from within. When we began to seek answers on how to defeat this stronghold, he turns up the pressure and will do everything in his power to keep us discouraged and naive to the damage this stronghold can cause. Satan hates us because God loves us. Satan cannot let go either.

"No power in the sky above or in the earth below—indeed, nothing in all creation will ever be able to separate us from the love of God that is revealed in Christ Jesus our Lord" Romans 8:39 (NLT). God gave us the ability to choose because He desires fellowship with us. God's desire for us to choose to love Him is no different than the desire we have for our own children to love us. We desire for our children to love us by choice, not because we force them to do so. How can you truly love someone if you are being made to love? *"We love Him because He first loved us"* 1 John 4:19 (KJV). When we begin to understand God's love, we begin to love others in a way that doesn't allow unforgiveness.

Avoiding the Dark side

Not letting go of something places us in a stronghold that can consume our every thought. The darkness we create in our heart can sometimes go unnoticed. I have ministered to men who have been shocked and embarrassed by how simple, yet harmful the diagnosis of this stronghold can be. The good news is when a stronghold, such as letting go is exposed, many sufferers can gain a swift victory. The hardest part of letting go is unforgiveness, but once we identify the core issue, we can begin to apply God's word and seek His guidance in defeating this joy stealer.

Let's address some of the core issues regarding the inability of letting go.

Wanting all the Answers

I have ministered to some who no matter how hard you try to help them understand, they simply will not budge in their reasoning without a clear answer as to why things happen the way they do. At some point in our lives we must wrestle down the thought that some answers are simply not there for us to understand. Yes, sometimes evil can happen in our lives with no reason as to why. The death of a child, the loss of a job, a natural disaster, these things are tragic but we must realize nothing gets by God and everything that happens on planet earth is controlled and supervised by Him.

What we see as a tragedy, God sees as a part of a bigger picture. We must remember, not only is God a great Father, He is also an amazing teacher. He allows all things to happen, good and bad, to draw us closer to Him. Sometimes our tragedies become our ministries. I could write another book on the miracles I have witnessed in my little community alone. I have seen God's hand at work to the point I sometimes have to remind myself to not get complacent with what God has revealed to me.

Proving Ground

This world we live in is our proving grounds. Earth still exists because people need saving. God loves us so much that He is slow in destroying the earth. It is His will that none would perish and all would come to salvation. Why do we sometimes have sorrow or pain? So that we can help others from our experience who might not otherwise understand God's free gift. *"For our present troubles are small and won't last very long. Yet they produce for us a glory that vastly outweighs them and will last forever"* 2 Corinthians 4:17 (NLT).

One of the great lies from hell is "God will never give you something you can't handle." God will not only bring difficulty in our lives, He will break us because He knows what happens if we do not accept His eternal salvation. Death comes for us all. Is it not better to suffer on this earth the 60 or 70 years we have, than to live eternally separated from God?

God is Always in Control

Before he went home to heaven in 2005, Adrian Rogers told of a little plaque that sat on his desk which said "Adrian, relax. I've got everything under control. God." Every time Pastor Adrian would face difficulty in his life, his eyes would suddenly look up from his desk and he would see that little reminder from God. Sometimes we seek answers that are not there. What if the answers are there, but God knows they would hurt us more than the question? I have learned if I trust in God above all else, I can have peace in all circumstances. While I sometimes fail in my faith, I can assure you God has never let me down. He loves me and all of us that much.

There are two pieces of scripture I hang my heart on regarding those who are constantly searching for an answer they never seem to find. God says, "*For my thoughts are not your thoughts, nor are your ways My ways,' says the Lord. 'For as the heavens are higher than the earth, so are My ways higher than your ways, And My thoughts than your thoughts*" Isaiah 55:8-9 (NKJV). God is on a completely different spectrum of understanding and wisdom from us. He sees the end of every scenario before it takes place. This means we don't always need answers, but we always need to trust. The second piece of scripture I often go to when someone seeks an answer that can't seem to be found is Proverbs 3:5-6 "*Trust in the Lord with all of your heart and lean not on your own understanding; in all of your ways acknowledge Him, And He shall direct your path*" (NKJV). "Relax. I've got everything under control. God"

Cutting the cord

When I was in the early stages of ministry, some of my mentors would caution me on those who can literally suck the life out of you. Those people are the ones who always have problems or have the same problem that never goes away. Some people thrive on drama, create their own problems and actually get some sort of pleasure when others run to their rescue.

I had a man whom I ministered to who was dealing with a divorce which brought him to a major state of depression. He would work all day, yet had no home to go to because his wife took everything he had. He had no choice but to move in with his brother. It was his brother who reached out to me. When this man got home, he would turn out the lights in his room, close the curtains and just sat in the dark. He did this for days. It seemed no matter how much I attempted to help this man, there was never a breakthrough. There comes a time when we must accept the fact that we are unable to get through and professional help is required. In such a case I turn to a more experienced pastor and, depending on the situation, I may reach out to a Christian counselor on that person's behalf.

It's not that God cannot reach that person. It comes down to whether they truly want to be helped. We always have a choice. Until a person chooses to be helped, there is really nothing to do but pray that God will intervene. When we hand them off to a better suited minister or a professional, we must separate ourselves from the situation emotionally and move on to those we can help. 1 Corinthians 3:6 says "*I planted, Apollos watered; but God gave the increase*" (KJV). This is not only a verse that speaks of God's salvation, it also reminds us that it is God and God alone that gives the increase in every situation. We are only a vehicle God chooses to use. When we have done all we can for someone, we must care enough about that person to hand them off to someone more suited for them. We then must cut the cord and focus on others who are in need.

When getting involved we must always be on guard as to whether we need to take the lead in getting professional counseling or even contacting the police in some cases. The last thing we need is to carry the burden of not doing the right thing. When helping a friend, we must know our own limits. First, we must know that we aren't capable of saving anyone. Secondly, a Christian professional counselor has been trained for this scenario, so don't hesitate to call. Sometimes a state of depression can be so mind numbing that people cannot think for themselves.

I have seen situations where people not well versed in God's word try to minister and it does more harm than good. Use Godly knowledge based on facts. I have seen people who want to minister, but because they do not know scripture very well, they begin to use street knowledge in place of Godly wisdom. This is dangerous and can confuse those who do not know Christ. Remember only God's word carries the power to change lives. Most people are in predicaments because somebody didn't follow Godly counsel.

While using our testimony is a great tool, we need to be listeners first. Some people just need to talk. When we feel their need for spiritual ministry may be beyond our wisdom or knowledge, we need to call a pastor. Seeking knowledge beyond our own demonstrates wisdom and God will bless it.

Hidden benefits

We talk about those who we need to cut the cord with, but what if we are the attention seekers? The hidden benefit of not letting go or cutting the chord is that we get plenty of attention. If we do this, we are taking advantage of our friends. Be careful as a friend's compassion will eventually dry up. Nobody wants to be around people who are sad or in need all of the time. We have enough problems of our own without adding somebody else's bottomless pit of unsolvable issues. "Misery loves company" is only true when two people are together who like to complain all of the time. When we help others by pointing them to Christ, we are blessing them and all of those involved.

Control

There will be circumstances in life that will simply be out of our control. Give them to God and trust Him with the outcome. In the meantime, we can pray to Him and He will handle the rest. Remember one of the two greatest powers in the universe is prayer. Pray to God often, seek personal time with Him and His word.

Unforgiveness

Having unforgiveness in our hearts can be the greatest disruptive force on earth. I know people who carry such burden in their lives and they don't even realize it. Several years ago, there was an altercation between a friend and I that got physical. The issue was partially cleared up when I told him I forgave him, but I never wanted to see him again. I thought about that altercation everyday for the next year. I was unwilling to accept the fact that my pride played a part in it. I knew he was sorry for what happened. Then one day while sitting under the leadership of Pastor Dwayne Sumner, I heard a sermon on forgiveness. While he was preaching, a verse jumped off the page that has forever impacted my life. "*For if you forgive other people when they sin against you, your heavenly Father will also forgive you. But if you do not forgive others their sins, your Father will not forgive your sins*" Matthew 6:14-15 (NIV).

I was broken. I had realized the reason I carried so much animosity for this man was because in truth I never really forgave him. Pastor Dwayne went on to explain how God loves us in spite of who we are, and we are obligated to uphold the same standard towards others. After the sermon I gave Pastor Dwayne my usual man hug and as soon as I got to my car, I called my friend who I had not seen for almost a year. His answering machine took my message. Something told me he was actually listening in and was afraid of taking my call in fear I would say something to further hurt his feelings.

I went on to explain to the answering machine how I was wrong and that in truth I never really forgave him. I told my friend that from this moment on I unconditionally forgave him, and I asked him to do the same for me. The second I hung up the phone I felt as if a 100-pound weight had come off of my shoulders. I began to experience a freedom I have never felt. Robyn and I were not home from church very long before I heard a knock on the door. As Robyn opened the door, there stood my friend. The agony on his face revealed to me the sorrow he had been under for almost a year. We embraced with our tears flowing. From that moment on we began to rebuild a relationship that I would not trade for anything in the world. Today we have each other's back. I love him like a son and I know he loves me like a dad.

Sometimes we cannot understand how a hatred such as this begins, but what we do know is if we don't confront this sin God will not forgive us our sins. It really has nothing to do whether the other party forgives us or not. It has more to do with us releasing that burden and gaining the freedom to live in peace within our own heart. I believe when we unconditionally forgive someone, God in turn blesses us, because it blesses His heart to watch as His children forgive one another. I can say this because I am one who has received blessing upon blessing because of unconditional forgiveness.

How do we forgive?

Let it go! See unforgiveness for the joy thief this stronghold truly is. Deep down no one wants to carry the burden of unforgiveness. I cannot shake the feeling of the 100-pound weight coming off of my shoulders. Unforgiveness is nothing more than hate. Even if when the other person deserves it, hate and unforgiveness damages us more. Unforgiveness is a stronghold that should be purged from our lives. Unforgiveness is a jail sentence of solitary confinement we place on ourselves because usually the one we are holding a grudge against has no idea how we feel.

Photo by Kevin Carden

When someone I minister to has unforgiveness in their heart, I encourage them to confront the individual. I once had a lady who had unforgiveness in her heart from a situation that happened 10 years earlier. She found the person living in another town, called them and stated, "You possibly don't remember me, but you hurt me ten years ago and I just want you to know I forgive you."

Although the person did remember her, he was completely unaware he had hurt her. Since she was willing to confront the situation, she felt better and gained peace from an issue she carried for ten years. There may be an issue where the unforgiveness may be for a person who has since passed away. I know people who have visited the grave site, spoke to that person as if they were standing there and told them that they were forgiven. I know the deceased person didn't hear them, but God certainly did.

When physical, sexual or mental abuse, are involved, unconditionally forgiving someone can include keeping them at a safe distance. God says we must forgive them, but He does not want us placing ourselves in an unpredictable situation or in harm's way. God knows your heart. In a case such as this, pray to God for His peace and let Him know of the decision to forgive. He already knows our intentions and He will most assuredly bless us for it.

Confront the Sin

Having the inability of letting go or the inability to forgive someone is a spiritual stronghold. We must see it for what it is and not allow Satan to keep us in this situation. I would suggest starting a journal. Write down your experiences, especially the good ones. Make note of when God shows up and does His work inside of you. When pride or guilt of self gets in the way, go back and read about the times God showed up. It reminds us of our victories and will create peace and purpose. Leave nothing unwritten. Pray and ask God to grant the wisdom to forgive others. Place the power of forgiveness in the battle plan. Make it a chief weapon of attack. We cannot hate something we have chosen to love. Choose to love the action of forgiveness and watch the weight come off.

Seek Forgiveness

When we realize we have unforgiveness in our heart, we should seek those we have hurt along the way and seek their forgiveness. For that to be effective we must also forgive those who have trespassed against us. We must forgive what hurt us, but not forget what it taught us.

Answer the Call

Let go and let God. The pain will leave when we let go. We will never have true value of the moment until it becomes history. Answer the call. Forgive and then share with others how God forgave. We are His voice and every time we share His good news, He creates another opportunity for us to gain a brother or sister in Christ. He takes our mess and turns it into a message.

Finally

Forgiveness brings unimaginable freedom. Whatever we're holding on to, we must dismiss it! We have wasted too much time hating someone or some situation. We are not defined by what we've done or what's been done to us. If we follow Christ we are defined by His love.

1) What in your life do you feel you have trouble with letting go?
    _____
    _____
    _____

2) Do you have unforgiveness in your heart?_____
    Explain _____
    _____
    _____

3) Do you believe the world we live in is our proving grounds? _____
    Explain:_____
    _____
    _____

4) Do you believe God is always in control? _____
    Write down an instance in your life where you find this to be
    true: _____
    _____
    _____

5) In what areas in your life do you feel the need to cut the cord?
    _____
    _____

6) How do we forgive? _____
    _____
    _____

7) Do you have someone from your past you would like to offer the
    gift of forgiveness? _____
    Write down their name _____
    _____
    _____

CHAPTER ELEVEN

Lust

Of every stronghold listed in this book, nothing is more catered to in our culture than lust. Our lusts are well known and exploited by those in charge of movies, TV, advertising, internet, and social media. Most movies today promote some type of exploitation of a woman's body. Sex sells. Worldwide, pornography is reported to rake in anywhere from $57 billion to $100 billion dollars annually. In the United States alone, the porn industry generates more revenue than CBS, NBC and ABC combined. Pornography makes more money than all professional sports including the NFL, NBA and Major League Baseball.

According to the U.S. News and World Report "Americans spend more money at strip clubs than at Broadway, off- Broadway, regional and nonprofit theaters, the opera, the ballet and classical music performances combined."

In addition to the adult porn industry, the perverse world of pornography branches out into obverse categories which are disturbing and illegal. The FBI reports those who engage in the production and distribution of child pornography come from all walks of life and represent varied ages, races, occupation, and educational levels. Typically, their crimes are carried out on the dark web-where they can remain anonymous. The FBI's analysis of one particularly egregious website found that it hosted approximately 1.3 million images depicting children being subjected to violent sexual abuse.

Today sexual orientation is no longer kept in the closets, but rather is flaunted in the face of the American church with gay pride week and

Disney World making a day of celebration for those who practice what the Bible calls an abomination.

For many years the most often quoted verse in the Bible has been John 3:16. Now the most quoted verse in the Bible, or should I say misquoted verse, is "Thou shall not judge." Many people use this verse as an attempt to silence their critics, interpreting Jesus' meaning as "You don't have the right to tell me I'm wrong". However, there is much more to this passage than just these four words. When a non-believer attempts to bash Christians with this mis-quote, we find ourselves stuck because we don't know the scriptures well enough to defend our stance.

The verse actually says *"Judge not, that you be not judged. For with what judgment you judge, you will be judged; and with what measure you use, it will be measured back to you"* Matthew 7:1-2 (NKJV). The issue here is we confuse the actual act of judgment. This verse lets us know that the final judgement is reserved for God alone, but we are allowed to show discernment. To read Chapter Seven further reveals this truth *"Or how can you say to your brother, 'Let me remove the speck from your eye'; and look, a plank is in your own eye?"* Matthew 7:4 (NKJV).

"Do not give what is holy to the dogs; nor cast your pearls before swine, lest they trample them under their feet, and turn and tear you in pieces" Matthew 7:6 (NKJV). Jesus knew this scripture would often be misused by the non-believer. He warns us of what will happen when we don't know His words well enough to defend it. Is not God's word holy? Is not God's word as precious as pearls? Doesn't the non-believer tear us into pieces when they miss quote the very word of God and we aren't capable to defend it?

"If God does not judge America for our sin, then He owes Sodom and Gomorrah an apology" (Billy Graham). I am not playing judge and executioner, I am just holding God to His word. *"This is a trustworthy saying, and everyone should accept it: Christ Jesus came into the world to save sinners"* --and I am the worst of them all" 1 Timothy 1:15 (NLT).

My own prison

I did not understand the severity of lust until 1993 when I became involved in an extramarital affair that lasted almost three years. As a successful girls softball coach, I was very popular among the parents in our town. The divorced mothers especially respected me for the investment I was making in their girls' lives because most of their fathers were simply not engaged. Like many Americans, I claimed to be a Christian because I knew of God, but I had no real relationship with Him. I was mad at God because He let cancer take my father away. I knew adultery was wrong, but I needed some sort of release from my frustration. I had an adulterous affair to get back at God. To be honest, in the moment it seemed exciting and fun. I was excited by the thrill of the chase and keeping secrets from my wife. It gave me a rush.

Every time I would engage in my sin, I would come home feeling guilty until the next phone call for the next rendezvous would consume my every thought. I'll never forget that night when some inner force was moving me to tell my wife of the affair. Little did I know how the need of rush would affect my family. At the time my popularity at the ball field was such that several parents had asked me to run for City Council. However the more reckless I had become with my secrets, the more parents began to pull away. I began to pick up on the stares and the whispers behind my back. Although my children did not actually know of my affair, they suspected, and their friends began to talk behind their backs as well. I saw the stress my recklessness had put on my family, but I was so engulfed with lust that I didn't think it was causing irrevocable damage. I noticed the guys whom I thought would never break our code of silence began to back away as well.

One evening while lying in bed, I heard my dad's voice ask "Boy! What are you doing?" The voice was so loud and clear it literally caused me to roll out of my bed falling onto the floor. I do not believe dead people can come back to earth and talk to us, but I do believe God will use angels who will identify with us in a form or shape we are familiar with in order to get our attention or give us peace. When I got in trouble with my dad as a child, these were the very words that got my attention. When he said "Boy, what are you doing" this usually meant that there were bad times coming.

From that moment on I realized the pain and stress I had brought upon my family. I knew the only way to heal my family was to get out of town where my children would not feel the stares and whispers at the ball field. My children had many good friends. Robyn had never lived anywhere other than Jacksonville Beach. Uprooting my family was a great hardship on them, but I believed with all my heart it was the right move.

I'll never forget the day we drove away from my children's childhood home. The U-Haul was packed. It was pouring down rain and as my children got into my wife's car, I sat behind the U-Haul on the back bumper and cried the most uncontrollable cry I had ever cried in my life. The embarrassment I had brought upon my family and myself was almost too much to bear. Even as I write these words, the pain brings back the emptiness, brokenness and the weight of guilt that was so strong that it still makes it hard to breathe. I had created my own prison. Why am I writing this, Lord? Why have you placed this burden on me to tell my story and being forced to relive it all over again? Will this chapter help someone? Will my grandchildren read this and forever see me differently? Am I back there, again, living in the prison I have created for myself?

God is Always There

After we moved, I intentionally didn't make friends for a decade. I didn't trust people anymore. We went to church out of habit and uttered all the rituals. My children demonstrated great resilience as they began to make new friends. I brought travel softball (The Nassau County Firebirds) to Fernandina Beach. It wasn't until twelve years later that I began to see the movement of God in my life. On January 8, 2006, a light came on within my mind. God got my attention "Who is this Jesus? Why did He die for me?"

As I studied the Word I began to understand God was there all along. God was there during the affair. God was there when my father died. I have a story that needs to be told. I need to share the heartache. I need to share the pain, the brokenness, the loneliness, and the pain that I brought upon my family. Today when I preach, people come to me and express their appreciation from the passion in which I speak. As shared in the beginning of this book, I am not a formally educated preacher. I preach from pain. I am passionate because I do not want to see others make the same mistakes I have made. I want men to understand that when these mistakes are made, it is important to realize the same God who never left me or forsook me, loves you. God is in the business of taking our mess and turning it into a message. *"In Him we have redemption through His blood, the forgiveness of our trespasses, according to the riches of His grace"* Ephesians 1:7 (ESV).

God's Design

Statistically, adulterous affairs cause divorce. When the trust of intimacy between a man and a woman is broken, most marriages (Christian or non-Christian) do not make it. Sometimes the person who committed the offense ends up going from one relationship after another because they continue to commit the same offense expecting different results. Just because man begins to accept a lifestyle that is contrary to God's will, doesn't make it okay. There is an order in which life happens in this universe and it's by God's design. When we go against God's design, it goes against His nature as well as the natural order of the universe in which He created. That is called sin and sin has consequences.

Origin of Lust

Lust is all a part of the fall of man. When Adam stood by and allowed Eve to be swayed by the devil in Genesis 3, he demonstrated a lack of leadership, lack of discipline and laziness. He gave up his very control of the natural order God had placed in him and gave Satan power over the earth. Just like Adam did not understand the ramifications of standing by and doing nothing, neither do we understand the ramifications of our own lack of discipline and laziness when we commit the same type of self-indulgent act. We do not realize the lives we are hurting because of our lack of leadership and discipline. Neither did Adam at the time understand the curse he brought upon the common man that exists today. That's why Jesus is referred to as the second Adam. What Adam gave away and lost, Jesus restores and conquers, but only when we repent from the way of the world and learn the real meaning of love.

Lust versus Love

Nowhere in life is the power of love better understood than through our relationship with Christ. Concerning our relationship with our human partner, are we in love or are we in lust? Ever hear of "Love at first sight?" That is not love. Love is a choice. How do we make a choice to love someone if we do not know their character, mind and heart? When "love at first sight" happens, we are falling for appearance, mannerisms, or sex appeal.

There have been instances where "love at first sight" lasts a lifetime, but in such cases these people were lucky. These same statistics of a "love at first sight" lasting a lifetime are about the same as winning the lottery. They gambled and won. Divorces happen today because we judge our partners based on how good they are in bed, rather than the compatibility of living life together. The Bible is very clear that a sexual relationship should only be between man and woman after they are united in marriage. In the world we live in today, we have gotten the cart before the horse.

Thrill of the Chase

Sweaty palms. Racing heart. Seductive smiles and side glances. We can refer to this as "the thrill of the chase." Most of this happens when we pursue a woman for the purpose of sex. We put the cart before the horse and buy into the lie that we must also be compatible in other areas of our life as well. Most of the time heartache follows as well as a failed marriage. I cannot begin to tell you how many men I have ministered to who have made the comment, "I thought I knew her." In order to avoid this disappointment we should exercise courtship before becoming eternally committed.

What is Courtship

A lasting marriage begins in the very early stages of dating. It is certainly okay to be sexually attracted to a woman. God designed us to desire a woman, but demonstrating respect for her speaks volumes to a woman regarding who you are as a man. Ask her out on a date, but demonstrate respect for her by not making sexual advances. Men who attempt to take advantage of a girl for sex are self-centered and lack self-control. When our sexual desires control us, this is sin.

Unfortunately, some women will feel the peer pressure and give in to our advances. They end up sharing with a scavenger what they should be sharing with their lover on their honeymoon. This happens because fathers do not sit down with their son's and explain how to treat a woman. The father of the daughter is often not present in their lives and the girl is searching to be accepted or looking to fill that void. If we don't love our daughters enough, she will allow someone else. If we don't love and teach our kids, nobody else will.

Courting a young lady earns respect of families and will be remembered. If you find both of you do not get along or have different thoughts regarding major life choices and events, there is no harm in breaking up and moving on. This gives the opportunity to become friends before emotions take control. This can lead to a more rewarding and peaceful life with the right partner. I have known young men who honored God with their bodies and did not engage in sexual intercourse until after marriage. I can tell you there is a sense of accomplishment and wisdom in their daily walk. The love between them seem to be much stronger than most.

If you are currently un-married and sexually active, remember God is a God of second chances. Pray, confess your sin to God, repent and ask God for forgiveness. He will forgive you. Abstain from sex and honor God and your future wife with your body.

Why is Sex Fun?

God created sex to be fun! When we can fight the urge and learn abstinence, the relationship will flourish beyond imagination. God will bless obedience. God intended sex to be the great reward between man and woman who are united in marriage.

True Intimacy

God created sexual desire. God is so perfect in His design that He created a need for intimacy in both man and woman. In His perfecting, He created both to have a need to be fulfilled in different ways. When intimacy is satisfied according to God's design, a loving relationship between man and woman is to be expected. Love and respect is demonstrated in every sense of our being. The Bible is full of instructions for, not only satisfying the body, but the mind as well. When this happens, the stronghold of lust will be defeated.

King Solomon was the wisest man who ever lived. He wrote the book "Song of Solomon" about God's gift of courtship, sex, and intimacy.

> *"How beautiful and pleasant you are, O Loved one, with all of your delights. Your stature is like a palm tree, and your breasts are like its clusters. I say I will climb the palm tree and lay hold of its fruit. Oh, may your breasts be like clusters of the vine, and the scent of your breath like apples, and your mouth like the best wine. It goes down smoothly for my beloved, gliding over lips and teeth. I am my beloved's, and his desire is for me"* Song of Solomon 7:6-10 (ESV).

Men and Women are wired different

Men are visual. They see, they want. Physical intimacy leads to emotional intimacy. Most of our relationships as men are built around activity. We feel connected to our co-workers, teammates, etc. A man feels connected to his wife through sex. Men are fixers. When we have an urge for sex, we need to fix the problem. This is contrary to how a woman enjoys sex.

Women are relational. The greatest way to initiate sex with your wife is to stimulate her mind. This is the way God designed her. The way a woman is aroused is when we pay attention to them. Turn off the T.V., look into her eyes, listen to her, ask about her day. Perform random acts of kindness without her asking, and without seeking credit. When we point out our act of kindness, she immediately knows there was an ulterior motive. This destroys the notion of love and violates her trust. A woman's natural instinct to nurture will be exhibited when we demonstrate love while expecting nothing in return. She already knows how much you enjoy sex. She will naturally desire to nurture your needs. Being relational with your wife earns her affection.

What Every Woman Needs

I once served as director of men's ministry at a church that had a congregation of over 1,500 people. I gave a survey among the women of every age and culture in an attempt to understand where men lacked the most in relationships. The response was staggering. Many women wanted to feel safe, secure, and more cared for, but the number one need was trust.

This is why the stronghold of lust is Satan's favorite tool to use in breaking up marriages. All women have a need to feel safe in a relationship. Women need to feel secure. Women need to have a productive relationship with a man and they want to feel protected. All these factors hinge on one single denominator, TRUST. When a man turns to another woman for sexual pleasure, our wife's ability to trust is destroyed. Satan wins.

Women want out of the marriage because they cannot compete with an airbrushed model on an internet porn site. They cannot feel secure any longer in their own home because they don't know where their husband's loyalty lies. The wife's trust is obliterated because if her husband is willing to violate the sacredness of their bedroom, where else is he being untrustworthy?

Satan Loves Lust

Our eyes are a window to our soul. I believe Satan's primary focus when it comes to relationships are first and foremost on the man because man is easier to sway when it comes to temptation. All we need is a beautiful woman on television trying to sell hamburgers and the struggle starts.

Satan also knows women are relational. Look again in Genesis 3 how Satan reasoned with Eve in order to coerce her to sin.

"Now the serpent was more cunning than any beast of the field which the Lord God made. And he said to the

woman, 'Has God indeed said, you shall not eat of every tree in the garden? And the woman said to the serpent, 'We may eat the fruit of the trees of the garden, but of the fruit of the tree which is in the midst of the garden God said, 'You shall not eat it, nor shall you touch it, lest you die.' Then the serpent said to the woman, 'You shall not surely die. For God knows that in the day you eat of it your eyes will be opened, and you will be like God, knowing good and evil" Genesis 3:1-5 (NKJV).

Since the beginning of time, man has attempted to use logic or reason as a way to take advantage of a woman in order to satisfy his own desires just as Satan did in Genesis 3. Satan hates God. And since we are God's most prized possession, Satan hates us. Satan knows he can't hurt God, so what does he do? He hurts what God loves. Us.

Adam stood by and watched as Satan manipulated his wife. *"Husbands, in the same way be considerate as you live with your wives, and treat them with respect as the weaker partner and as heirs with you of the gracious gift of life, so that nothing will hinder your prayers"* 1 Peter 3:7 (NIV).

When Peter calls our wives the weaker partner he means from a standpoint of physical strength. Men are called to be the headship of the home, but this is because of the gifts God has placed in us to lead. God has given both the husband and wife different gifts and strengths made to complement one another regarding the family. Men and women are both created in God's image to express His fullness. When we apply these gifts together, we will witness the great reward God has created in the family.

The Best Sex

God intended sex to be between one husband and one wife. When we are focused on our own desires we often never give marriage a fighting chance. Marriage is a constant work in progress. Forgiveness must be at the forefront of every circumstance because a real marriage takes place between two imperfect, sinful people. I can tell you from my heart, I am a man who has dealt with the issue of lust all of my life. I can also tell you I have never experienced sex the way I have since I accepted Jesus as Lord over my life. Sin numbs our senses. When we read God's word, we discover sex as it should be under the authority of God.

When we exhibit real love towards our wives and engage in conversation of what the marriage is supposed to look like in God's eyes, our sex lives will soar. I have worked with many men in the area of understanding sex. If you want to have the greatest sex of your life, invite God into the bedroom. Literally sit down on your bed and pray hand in hand with your wife and ask God to bless the union that is about to take place. Guys, I promise it works. When sex is experienced under the authority of God, lust is destroyed, and love finds its place in the arms of your help mate.

The Stronghold of Lust

Men, our greatest weapon against the spiritual stronghold of lust is the Word of God. Using our spiritual toolbox is our greatest deterrent in keeping lust at bay. We are designed to desire sex. The difference between real sexual pleasure and sexual sin is whose eyes we see the act of sex through. Do we see sex through the eyes of Satan, or do we see sex through the eyes of God? In a fallen world, lust will be an everyday battle, but one that can we won everyday. Most men simply do not know how to speak of lust as a stronghold or how to confront the sin. Men today see sex as a crown to wear and a topic of conversation around the water cooler at work.

No man wants to think of lust as a stronghold. Society shoves lust down our throat like we need it to survive, but the opposite is true. Sharing our battles of lust with other men brings this stronghold into the light.

Several years ago, I was serving under one of the greatest men pastors I have ever known, Pastor Ben Hall. He had a great idea to start a bi-weekly men's study called "The Locker Room." We had close to 50 men sign up for our first class. Ben's idea was to take the men through a book called *Every Man's Battle* by Fred Stoeker and Steve Arterburn. This is one of the best books on the market for dealing with sexual temptation. After Ben made the introduction as to what our area of study was going to be, we had less than 20 men show up at our next meeting.

Confronting the sin

We must confront this trust stealing, family destroying, stronghold of lust head on. We must bring this stronghold out into the light. I have found as hard as the topic of lust is to talk about among men, how quickly we find out that men will open up regarding their own lust issues when we are willing to open up with our own confession. To succeed, we must find a trusted group of men. As I have said from the very beginning, the key to enjoying a great journey in life is to surround ourselves with other Godly men.

Seek counsel from a pastor regarding lust. Depending on the depth of the stronghold a Christian counselor may be needed. Using someone who better understands the spiritual realm will be an advantage. I recommend seeking a Christian counselor who will attack the problem spiritually and emotionally.

Our wives will be the key to maintaining success regarding the stronghold of lust. Since women work differently, they can learn about the stronghold of lust which will allow them to support us. Of course we must be careful on how we approach the subject of involving our wives with this. They, too, have been educated by the world regarding sex. Most women see sex today as a necessity for men. They have no idea the joy that can come from experiencing intimacy through the eyes of God.

Chances are the way in which our wives view sex is determined by the burden we as husbands have placed on them. The Christian wife should, hopefully, be willing to work through the process since we can point her to the truths contained in the word of God. If our wife doesn't share our faith, this will be much harder. With much prayer and practice, this could be used to help win her to the faith.

The greatest way to defeat lust is to manage our sex lives. For singles who have a need for sex, I recommend getting started on the courtship of a woman. Abstinence must be practiced until marriage occurs because the joy that will come by remaining faithful to God during this process will bring a lifetime of self-worth and blessings. The Apostle Paul never married, but had a good point of view on sex.

"Now to the unmarried and the widows I say; It is good for them to stay unmarried, as I do. But if they cannot control themselves, they should marry, for it is better to marry than to burn with passion" 1 Corinthians 7:8-9 (NIV).

When it comes to educating your wife about a man's battle with lust, it is also important to be educated about women. The best book outside of the Bible that can help the both of you understand what makes a man and a woman tick is *Love and Respect* by Doctor Emerson Eggerichs. Proper education will bring better understanding thus making our sexual relationship with our wives much better.

The woman needs to be educated that our sex drive is quite different than hers. Men have needs, men have urges. Where women today believe it's just a guy wanting to fool around in fact goes much deeper than we realize. Men have urges where sex is needed to have relief. God wired us this way. I disagree with the standard that Catholic priests cannot marry. If they can follow in the footsteps as Paul is one thing, but the Bible is very clear regarding the union between man and woman. This also may give an answer as to why some priests are walking away from their religion. The Apostle Paul speaks of this urge in the verse we just read. In 1 Corinthians 7:9 talks about "passion." Most men naturally burn with passion. Sometimes we don't need to see a picture of a scantily-clad woman to get our motor going. All we need to do is wake up from a nap. Women block a man's need when they choose not to engage in sex.

The reason this happens is not because the wife is denying her husband, they simply do not view sex the same way a man does. Men are visual, women are relational. When our wives understand that being intimate with them is a part of how God designed us, the wife will naturally be more conscience to our needs because women are also nurturers. When we are rejected by our wives, that passion that lives inside us begins to tap into our sin nature. Regrettably, no matter how loyal a husband may be, these urges may create wandering eyes. This is why the best way to manage our sex life is by having sex with our wives whenever we have the urge.

"But since sexual immorality is occurring, each man should have sexual relations with his own wife, and each woman with her own husband. The husband should fulfill his marital duty to his wife, and likewise the wife to her husband. The wife does not have authority over her own body but yields to her husband. In the same way, the husband does not have authority over his own body but yields to his wife. Do not deprive each other except perhaps by mutual consent and for a time, that you may devote yourselves to prayer. Then come together again so that Satan will not tempt you because of your lack of self-control" 1 Corinthians 7:2-5 (NIV).

It really can't be any clearer than the scripture we just read. One of the ways I helped myself with my issue of lust was by sitting down with my wife and explaining the weakness of a man. With God's guidance, I was able to help her to understand a man's need to be intimate. When my wife began to understand this, she became more attentive to my needs. This kept my urges from becoming sinful. We must also give as much back to our wives as they are giving to us. A woman is relational and the giving must go both ways. The more you attend to her needs, the more she will attend to yours. This makes a regular marriage into an awesome marriage.

Never forget that God is the Master of life. Our relationship with Him must be intimate if we have any chance to have an intimate relationship with our wives. No stronghold can be broken down without prayer and the Word.

Seek Forgiveness

With all the pain I have caused my family due to my anger and lust issues, I marvel at how my wife can still desire to live life with me after 40 years of marriage. This is evidence of a mighty God who can heal and restore. When we commit sin against another person, we must seek forgiveness regardless of the outcome. I have seen many marriages repaired and lives restored by the act of forgiveness. Sometimes we have a hard time taking that step of obedience, but God is faithful.

Seeking forgiveness from the person we have offended will help heal our pain as well. It's not their response that is most important, but rather God's response.

I know Robyn loves me. I know her inner strength far surpasses most women in that rather than kick me to the curb when I sinned against her, she sought God in restoring what she had a hard time understanding. I will always believe God pulled me from the depths of hell not because of anything I did, but rather because Robyn constantly prayed for me during the darkest years of my life. She chose to fight for our marriage even when I was not willing to do so. I could only wish some of the families I have attempted to help along the way would have had Robyn's obedience regarding the act of forgiveness. God honored her desire to forgive my sin and that is why we have such a great relationship today.

The first One we must seek forgiveness from is the very One we've sinned against, our God, because only He has the power to restore life to an otherwise dead marriage. Whether is it pornography, a wandering eye, or an affair, we need to seek forgiveness from our wives, as well. There will be some rough times when the truth comes out, trust me, but with an omnipotent God on our side, marriage can be restored.

I can't leave this chapter without offering some advice between the Christians and the Gay community. With love and humility I have to say that God does not approve of a gay lifestyle. He does not approve of an adulteress lifestyle either. God has the final say regarding the universe. If we are so unforgiving on the gay community, how are they going to discover Jesus?

Some Christians do not want those who live in this type of sin attending their church. Is the drug addict sitting next to us any different? What about the father who just met with his mistress the night before? It's all sin, right? A successful church would be a place where a woman would have to watch her purse when placed in the pew because someone may try to steal it. Isn't that the kind of place Jesus spent a great deal of His time? Isn't this where we Christians should be? Instead church today has become a social gathering, rather than a hospital for the lost.

I would welcome someone who is living a gay lifestyle into my church. I would want to get to know them because I hurt for them. I hurt for them because I know God hurts for them. My prayer would be to get to know them and once they got to know me, the animosity and the walls would come down which would make them more responsive to the Gospel. The "cure" for homosexuality isn't heterosexuality, it is Jesus.

I believe many who practice a gay lifestyle do so because they are accepted and not judged by others who practice the same sin. We all want to feel accepted or wanted. In retaliation against mom and dad or the Christian community, many homosexuals have become bold in promoting their lifestyle. Others are just plain lost and have no desire to know truth. They are so badly wrapped around Satan's finger that they don't even realize it. I believe many Christians go about this entire issue wrong. We either turn the other cheek thinking we are doing so according to scripture, yet in reality we are weak minded and don't like confrontations. Turning the other cheek is done in strength. The non-Christian community sees this action as weakness as well, but we must boldly stand behind God's word.

I wish other Christians would stand up for God rather than hide behind the four walls of their church and just preach to one another all day. God hates sin in all forms because it separates us from Him. A homosexual lifestyle is no different. *"You shall not lie with a male as with a woman; it is an abomination"* Leviticus 18:22 (NKJV). Other verses where the Bible is speaking on a gay lifestyle can be found in Romans 1:26-27, Jude 1:5-8, 1 Timothy 1:8-11, Leviticus 20:13.

Answer the call

Whether our weakness is sneaking on an internet porn site, being gay, having an extra marital affair, having sex outside the realm of marriage, it is a sin and sin separates us from a loving God. Lust is a spiritual stronghold and if we do not address this issue in our own lives whether it be from a generational curse or a learned behavior, our children will be the ones who will be left to break the chain of bondage. We must not leave this sickness to be confronted by our children, we must answer the call.

Answering the call is to go and share our story with others in hopes of leading them to Christ. We can use our stories to build a bridge to His story. I know men who are now sharing their stories of how God saved them, as well as their marriage from the spiritual stronghold of lust. I also know some formerly gay men who are now living in victory and enjoying the journey of faith. All of them have sought forgiveness and all of them have been forgiven and living lives to the fullest.

I pray for those who have been unable to grant forgiveness and have moved on. My prayer is they can learn to understand God's greatest gift. For those who have began their journey in faith, they have an eternal glory that awaits them, not to mention the freedom of bondage while here on this earth.

Photo by Kevin Carden

DISCUSSION

1) What are your thoughts on the newest often quoted verse in the bible "Thou shall not judge"? _____ _____ _____ _____

2) What are your thoughts on Lust versus Love? _____ _____ _____ _____

3) Do you believe love is a choice? _____ And when does love stop being a choice? _____ _____ _____ _____

4) Have you ever pursued a girl and enjoyed "the thrill of the chase" _____ _____ _____ _____

5) Have you actively courted a girl? _____ And what is the difference between Courting and the thrill of the chase? _____ _____ _____ _____

6) Men are visual. Do you agree with this statement? _____ Explain._____ _____ _____

7) Women are relational. Do you agree with this statement? _____ Explain._____ _____ _____

8) Have you ever experienced a situation where you know a female who you believe was taken advantage of either by yourself or someone else? _____
Explain._____
_____
_____

9) Name some of the random acts of kindness you have exhibited for your wife or your girlfriend? _____
_____
_____
_____

CHAPTER 12

Pride

Pride comes before the fall.

This is a quote accepted by Christians as scripture and by non Christians as well. What if I told you this quote is not in the Bible? The Bible actually says, *"Pride goes before destruction, And a haughty spirit before the fall"* Proverbs 16:18 (NKJV). While the quotes are similar, being biblically accurate is important to us and God. *"You shall not add to the word which I am commanding you, nor take away from it, that you may keep the commandments of the Lord your God which I command you"* Deuteronomy 4:2 (NASB). God states this same warning in Deuteronomy 12:32 and in Revelation 22:18. One little word can matter a great deal. This is why we must be careful to understand God's word because of its convicting as well as healing power.

What is pride

Pride is a spiritual stronghold used by Satan to destroy relationships. God hates pride *"To fear the Lord is to hate evil; I hate pride and arrogance, evil behavior and perverse speech"* Proverbs 8:13 (NIV). To understand the definition of pride only requires further study of this verse. Let's look at the three key words found in this passage: arrogance, evil behavior and perverse speech.

Arrogance - Is an offensive display of superiority or self-importance. It is an overbearing pride. It's an over exaggeration of one's worth. *"I will punish the world for it's evil, and the wicked for their iniquity; I will halt the arrogance of the proud and will lay low the haughtiness or the terrible"* Isaiah 13:11 (NKJV).

Evil behavior - is being vindictive, abusive, and completely selfish. Our goodness is squelched by an evil nature. There is little regard for religion or the fear of the law. *"Woe to those who call evil good and good evil, who put darkness for light and light for darkness, who put bitter for sweet and sweet for bitter"* Isaiah 5:20 (NKJV).

Perverse speech - When evil resides in the heart, it will be exposed through perverse speech. This is not limited to dirty jokes and curse words. This is any comment that is contrary to the truth and God's word. *"Keep your mouth free of perversity; keep corrupt talk far from your lips"* Proverbs 4:24 (NIV).

Arrogance, *proud* and *haughty* are mentioned over 200 times in the Bible. Before I knew Christ, I was extremely prideful. Back in high school I was better at baseball than football, but I liked football more because of the contact. I suffered from anger issues and through football, I was able to vent my daily frustrations. I had a reputation for recklessness and throwing my body around. Although I had the physical ability to play college ball, I had brittle bones. Every year I would suffer some sort of injury that limited my playing time. I broke my left hand on the first play of a game my junior year. I was the center and snapped the ball with my left hand, but my pride would not allow me to remove myself from the game.

I was not the best student either. I was too proud to ask for help on my class work, thus ended up never playing a down of college ball because I was not smart enough to do the college work. I was a good athlete, but not good enough for some college to overlook my failure in the classroom. All along, everyone was telling me I could have excelled in baseball. I could have passed on college life and have played in the minor leagues, but my pride made me focus on football. I would ignore the baseball coaches and friends who told me to play dual sports. I did not want practice time on the diamond to interrupt my training on the football field. In the end, I let pride steal my dreams.

We all deal with pride at some point in our lives. Is our pride nothing more than a passing thought? A bad habit? Does it consume every thought? More men deal with a consuming pride than we realize. A pride that consumes us is a stronghold. When we make pride a habit, we are often aware of this shortcoming and absolutely need to address this issue. When we have a stronghold of pride we don't even know we have the sickness. Yes, pride is a sickness.

Pride in Ministry

I had a man I didn't know contact me and tell me his wife served him with divorce papers.

She demanded that he get professional help or she would leave him. I've ministered to men who were not members of the church before, so it was not unusual that I did not recognize his name. He said it was very important that we meet at the church at a time when no one else was around because many people knew him, and he did not want to be seen with me because of my position with the community as a minister.

My typical meeting style with strangers would be in a public restaurant until I got comfortable with them. I thought to myself I better meet with him when someone was at the church in case this guy was mentally unstable.

I met him, took him to a private office and begin to listen to his story. What he said almost dropped me out of my chair. He began to tell me for over 30 years he had been married to the same woman yet he openly engaged in porn, had countless affairs, and every time his wife would confront him over his sinful lifestyle, he would tell her "I pay the bills in this house. I own this house, put food on the table and clothes on your back. I provide all of this for you. It's none of your business what I do with my life." I just sat there with my mouth wide open. I was hoping and praying this was some kind of sick joke. After a minute he looked at me and said, "Well aren't you going to say something?"

I replied "Sir, you are an idiot." I then asked, "If you are so convinced you are right, why are you here?"

"I thought you'd agree with me and talk to my wife," he said, "I am here because she said I cannot come back home until I started going to church."

I asked, "Do I know your wife?"

"Oh yes" he said, "She attends this church".

For the next half hour, I shared truth with this man. I normally exhaust every effort to save a marriage and avoid the thought of divorce, but in this case I explained to him according to scripture his wife had every right to divorce him. I told him I was surprised she had put up with him for 30 years. His response after 30 minutes of me not taking a breath was "I am offended that you call me an idiot."

"Well sir then, you're a moron" I said. To my surprise he showed up to church the next Sunday and went on to become a regular member. The marriage was repaired.

Pride is a feeling of deep pleasure derived from one's own personal satisfaction in their achievements. Pride is also a sickness found in people who possess an attitude that exhibits conceit, egotism, vanity etc. It is an inward emotion that can easily offend others and carries with it a false sense of one's own self-worth. This type of thinking creates a false sense of superiority over others.

Humility

God says He hates pride and loves humility all throughout His word. *"When pride comes, then comes disgrace, but with the humble is wisdom"* Proverbs 11:2 (ESV). *"For everyone who exalts himself will be humbled, and he who humbles himself will be exalted"* Luke 14:11 (ESV).

We begin to see God more clearly when we choose to be humble. When we are full of pride, we simply cannot see God moving in our lives because we are too self-centered to allow anything else in. When we walk humbly we began to feel His love as well as witness the work of God all around us. When we read the word of God, we begin to feel closer to Him and we can see His grace more clearly. When we do not read His word, we begin to drift and can very easily fall back into our prideful ways. The greatest way to confront this stronghold is to begin doing acts of kindness.

The greatest act of humility can be seen in the upper room when Jesus (the Son of God), begins washing the feet of His disciples.

> *"It was just before the Passover Festival. Jesus knew that the hour had come for Him to leave this world and go to the Father. Having loved His own who were in the*

world, He loved them to the end. The evening meal was in progress, and the devil had already prompted Judas, the son of Simon Iscariot, to betray Jesus. Jesus knew that the Father had put all things under His power, and that he had come from God and was returning to God; so, He got up from the meal, took off His outer clothing, and wrapped a towel around His waist. After that, He poured water into a basin and began to wash His disciples' feet, drying them with the towel that was wrapped around Him. He came to Simon Peter, who said to Him 'Lord, are you going to wash my feet?' Jesus replied, 'You do not realize now what I am doing, but later you will understand." John 13: 1-7 NIV.

Jesus went on to explain in John 13:16 that no servant was greater than his master and no messenger is greater than the one who sent him. He did not have to perform this act of love just for those in attendance, but as an example for all to follow.

With humility we can find peace. When we have a stronghold of pride, we must practice humility. When we walk humbly we get the respect and self worth we are craving. This is pleasing to the Lord. *"Sitting down, Jesus called to the Twelve and said, 'Anyone who wants to be first must be the very last, and servant to all"* Mark 9:35 (NIV).

Confront the Sin

Having like minded men in your life is the key. Share with them your stronghold of pride. Ask them to pray for you and hold you accountable. Drench your stronghold in prayer. Ask God to take this stronghold away. If the stronghold of pride persists, then recognize this pride as the thorn in your side according to 2 Corinthians 12:7-10. Be disciplined in Bible reading, meditation and prayer. Ask for help from a Christian counselor who can help us better understand the stronghold of pride.

Seek Forgiveness

First and foremost, ask your Lord and Savior for His forgiveness. His forgiveness is the one that matters most. Work to understand that we have caused harm to someone with our selfish desires. Seek them out and ask for forgiveness. An act of humbleness is always respected. Asking forgiveness is humility in its purest sense and has more to do with us than anyone else. The most powerful act we can perform ourselves is to forgive someone of their trespass. Allow someone else to experience this power by forgiving you.

Answer the Call

Share how God has delivered you from the stronghold of pride. I guarantee you everybody deals with issues of pride. Some don't even realize they have a pride issue. Be a light in a dark world. Be willing to exhibit the power of humility through sharing how God rescued you from yourself. Use your story to build a bridge to His story which has the power to set us free from the bondage of spiritual strongholds. This will cause Satan to lose his grip on another person who might otherwise bust hell wide open.

Thankfully, God saves people like you and me. I know the best place for anyone to be is in church hearing the word of God, but most people today do not go to church. A lot of this has to do with our own arrogance. We might be the only representation of Jesus someone else may see all day. You have more power within your testimony than any pastor can have on any given Sunday because you are walking the same streets of every sinner. You do not have to be an educated or influential speaker to get people's attention. All you have to be is a sinner saved by grace. Moses had an issue of speech. Jonah was a terrible preacher, but look at how many people came to know God because of their efforts.

Photo by Kevin Carden

1) Pride can be a mere passing thought. Pride can be a bad habit which is recognizable. But do you know someone who is consumed with pride? Yes_____No ____
Without mentioning names, explain what this person does that bothers you most. _____
_____
_____

2) Do you have issues with consuming pride? If so explain.
_____
_____

If you do not believe you have issues with consuming pride, explain why? you believe you do not._____
_____
_____
_____

3) What are your thoughts on arrogance? _____
_____
_____

4) What are your thoughts on evil behavior? _____
_____
_____

5) What are your thoughts on perverse speech? _____
_____
_____

6) Luke 14:11 says "anyone who exalts himself will be humbled, anyone who humbles himself will be exalted." What are your thoughts on this? _____
_____
_____

7) Regarding the stronghold of pride, what action are you willing to take whether for yourself or someone else? _____

_____

_____

_____

CHAPTER THIRTEEN

Maintaining Success

"A cloud by day to cover me, and fire by night to comfort me, my strength, my peace, to meet my every need, Before me, behind me, On every side You're there. You are my sun, You are my light, You're my hopes and dreams, Everything that's right, You calm the storms, You guard my life, And no matter where I choose to go. You are there. Cause You're my atmosphere".

I can think of no better way to explain a true relationship between our God and his creation than the song "Atmosphere" from Andy Chrisman on his 2004 album "One."

So here we are. The final chapter. My prayer is you were able to gain insight on a stronghold or strongholds you may be experiencing. I hope you have mounted up a battle plan on confronting this stronghold and exercised God's power in breaking the chain of this sickness. If you yourself are not dealing with a certain stronghold and your desire is to use this book to help you gain a better understanding and perhaps help others in defeating their strongholds, I pray you found this book helpful.

The most important lesson to learn from this book is when it comes to spiritual warfare is no human on earth can defeat a stronghold on their own. Only God's power can release us from strongholds. I believe the best way to defeat any stronghold in your life must be done with these three steps.

- Confront the sin (Call the darkness into the light)
- Seek forgiveness (From God first and others whom you may have offended)
- Answer the call (Share your testimony and begin walking in victory)

If you do not attend a church, I recommend seeking out a good Christian church and surrounding yourself with Godly men who are willing to pour into you and hold you accountable. Once again if the church you are seeking does not have a men's ministry, look elsewhere. Men need men. Men need to be enlightened with biblical truth.

Paul, Barnabas, Timothy

Every man regardless of his knowledge of God's word must surround himself with other Godly men. When we do this our journey becomes even more rewarding. We get to experience life changing relationships and we ourselves have an opportunity to invest into others. Regardless of your knowledge of ministry. You have something to offer. Whether it is to simply listen or just being there for someone in need. We all need a Paul, a Barnabas and a Timothy in our lives.

Paul – Is a man who has good knowledge of the bible, one who is willing to take time to lead you and listen to you. His bible knowledge and wisdom can help you grow in the word and in life. A Paul is someone who is a realistic and Godly example for you.

Barnabas – Is a friend, an encourager. Someone who will be there for you during a time of need. A Barnabas is not a "yes man". He is willing to speak truth into your life. Someone who will call you out and hold you accountable when you get out of line. And trust me, we are not perfect. We will stumble from time to time.

Timothy – Timothy is someone who you can invest into. He may be younger and possibly does not have as many life experiences as you. What we may not realize is when we invest in a younger or less experienced individual, we receive great joy when we become a blessing to them. As for me, perhaps the greatest joy in my life from a personal perspective is when I am able to invest into others. You will find this will be true in your life as well. Maybe you are a Timothy?

That's okay. There is someone (perhaps a child) or a young man from a fatherless home you can pour into who can gain by your influence.

One of my former preachers, Jackie Hayes, once said "having a Paul, Barnabas and a Timothy in your life is like a three-legged stool. If one part is missing, the stool cannot support itself." When all legs are intact, we have a strong foundation from which to build a successful walk through manhood. Having someone in which we can seek guidance, someone in which we can experience life with and someone we can invest into creates a well-rounded cycle of Godly investments and can change the family dynamic where Godly men are leading their homes according to God's design.

Remember, authentic manhood is not about how much you already know, but rather how much you are willing to learn. My prayer is you have learned how to use your spiritual toolbox (the bible) in obtaining answers for the questions you seek. Know that no book on Earth is as full of knowledge, wisdom and answers as the Holy bible. All other books combined cannot compare to God's word. No other book can claim to be the "living, breathing word of God." The sole purpose of the Bible, Old Testament included, is geared to do one thing, to reveal, build and maintain a relationship with Jesus Christ.

There are times when we need to speak to God, perhaps we need to hear from God. I believe sometimes God says "no". Sometimes God says, "not yet". Regardless, how can we ask for an answer if we have no relationship with God? I believe one of the most important tools I learned as a young Christian was in a marriage class. A sweet lady once stated "If you ever want to talk to God? Pray. He hears our every prayer. If you ever want to hear from God? Read His word. We find our answers in His word."

Devote time for prayer and study

In order to begin a journey of maintaining success over a stronghold, we need to create a time of daily prayer and study. It is of extreme importance to read His word daily. Proof on this importance is to simply ask any seasoned Christian. They will tell you that when they read His word daily, they feel closer to God. When they do not read His word daily, they begin to drift back into their old self. I recommend that you select a time throughout the day and commit ten to twenty minutes to His word and prayer time. Even if you only read one chapter per day it will greatly strengthen your walk with Christ. The key is you must make this time the most important part of your day.

I personally recommended morning time because it's the first thing you will do every morning and it will create a good habit. I enjoy getting up early before everyone else, make a cup of coffee. As the coffee is brewing, I pray. After prayer I sit down with my coffee (just me and my bible) and read a chapter. I find God's word will tag along with me throughout the day. I feel more at peace and it really helps when the stress of the day wears on. Others prefer to devote their time during lunch breaks at work or just before bed. Personally, bedtime never works for me because I find it hard to focus on His word when I'm tired. I also know of others whose bible and prayer time are immediately after dinner.

Regardless of which you choose (morning, noon or evening), this must become a standard practice. Don't let anything interrupt your personal time with God. You never know when it could be that evil addiction attempting to get its foot back in the door of your mind and breaking up your personal time with God. *"Beware of false prophets, They come to you in sheep's clothing, but inwardly they are ferocious wolves."* Matthew 7:15 NIV.

If you find yourself having trouble establishing a personal prayer and study time, remember the *sixty-day battle plan*, as explained in Chapter Six. Commit yourself to sixty days of discipline with no lapse or break in this practice. This will create a good habit and will help develop discipline in this matter. Regarding the *sixty-day battle plan* in Chapter Six, I strongly recommend re-reading the section on "how to prepare for your *sixty-day battle plan*."

Remember, our willpower is like a muscle. Often, we start out with good intentions, but if we do not practice good habits and train our minds to be disciplined in reading the word and prayer time, we will become fatigued. Therefore establishing and practicing Godly habits is essential to our success.

"Be alert and of sober mind. Your enemy the devil prowls around like a roaring lion looking for someone to devour." 1 Peter 5:8. NIV. Be on guard my friend. When you turn from the darkness and begin living a

life of victory, our greatest enemy Satan will be on the prowl. He will do everything he can to discourage you from living a changed life. Remember *"No temptation has overtaken you except what is common to mankind, And God is faithful; He will not let you be tempted beyond what you can bear. But when you are tempted, He will also provide a way out so that you can endure it."* 1 Corinthians 10:13 NIV. Consider the fact that when you begin walking a life with Jesus and you become under attack must mean you are very important to Christ and He must have a plan for your life. Otherwise, why would Satan attempt to discourage you?

Taking back your family

Ever hear of the old cliché "a family who prays together, stays together". It doesn't matter where you've come from or what sin you have committed, once God has released you from the burden of sin, He has forgiven you. You have positioned yourself to begin living an abundant life as spoken of in the very beginning of this book. You do not have to wait until you become well versed in God's word before becoming a leader of your home. Being a good leader in the home requires four actions: love, humbleness, transparency, and setting the example

Love – Demonstrate love for those who are under your care by always placing their needs ahead of your own. Always correct in love and never through anger. Demonstrate your willingness to be the hands and feet for your family.

Humbleness – Practicing humbleness. Never strong arm a situation unless it has to do with protecting your family. But always think before you act. Allow a time of healing in the case you have hurt a member of your family. They may reject you at first, but they will begin to see you working for a better relationship with Christ as well as themselves will be the key.

Transparency – Be willing to admit your past failures and never back down from the new life God has given you. Always be truthful with your family. Let them see you pray. Never hide your failures and remind them you are not perfect, but you can point them to the One who never fails in that of Jesus Christ. You may slip up from time to time, but demonstrating transparency will help them to trust.

Setting the example – Let your family witness you reading your bible, let them witness you praying. Let them see you holding your wife's hand and demonstrating compassion and kindness to everyone. Let them witness you going to church and making new friends in that of like-minded men. Remember our eyes are a window to our soul. Let them see the life change in your heart.

Family devotion time

It is of extreme importance to create a time with the family where you take the lead and sit down with your wife and children and devote the same practice as you have made for yourself (a time of prayer and study).

God made you the headship of the home

You must set the example. Not only are you disciplining yourself to study time and prayer, teach your family the importance of their personal time with God. They may not like it at first, but when they see the change in you will be much more acceptable on their part. Remember, you do not have to be a bible scholar to lead a family bible study. All you need is to be one step ahead. I suggest purchasing a study bible. Many of the explanations will be contained on the same page as the scripture. This will help you better understand God's word. Initiate thought-provoking discussion with every member of your household and regardless of a child's age, no question should be deemed silly. Remember, CONVERSATION and DIALOGUE is the missing ingredient with every family. Turn off all T.V.'s and cell phones and commit to your family during this time.

When Satan cannot penetrate your faith, he will begin to attack those within your family and your friends. Be prepared, and under no circumstance relent from the task at hand. Always be willing to reach out to an accountability partner or your pastor for help in this matter. This is your family. The actions you take now will create a lifetime of wisdom and knowledge for the children whom you are the headship. *"You fathers, don't provoke your children to wrath, but nurture them in the discipline and instruction of the Lord."* Ephesians 6:4 WEB. *"Husbands, love your wives, just as Christ loved the church and gave Himself up for her."* Ephesians 5:25 NIV.

In closing, I am not a writer. I am not a professional counselor with a college degree hanging on my wall. What I am is a sinner saved by grace. For reasons I will never understand God stepped out of heaven and looked my way, He convicted me of my sin and gave me an opportunity of redemption. He does this for everyone because He loves us this much.

The only means I have for thanking Jesus for taking my place on the cross is to boldly proclaim Him and to share my testimony to whoever will listen. I never realized the awesome gift of life I would be able to live after I accepted His free gift of salvation. I thought it was only to save me for the future (after I die), What a joyful journey I have today while yet still living. I have shared many personal stories and have risked ridicule and hardship from many whom I love by writing this book. However, if one person can be motivated to seek Jesus from these words, then the risk I take is justified. Through my brokenness over this past decade, God has given me a great gift to be able to minister to hundreds of men. Through my journey I have created a plan that works, but everything here you read is worthless without application. The rest is up to you.

Allow me to echo the words of Apostle Paul who said: *"When I came to you, brothers, I didn't come with excellence of speech or of wisdom, proclaiming to you the testimony of God. For I determined not to know anything among you, except Jesus Christ, and Him crucified. I was with you in weakness, in fear, and much trembling. My speech and my preaching were not of persuasive words of human wisdom, but in demonstration of the Spirit and of power, that your faith wouldn't stand in the wisdom of men, but in the power of God."* 1 Corinthians 2:1-5 WEB.

Again, I thank you for taking time to read this book. Thank you for allowing me into your minds and your hearts. My prayer is everything stated in the book will be for the glory of God. I am truly honored to have written this book in hopes it will draw you closer to the One who is in the business of saving the lost. Always remember to use your own story to build a bridge to His story. His story is the only story who can save those who are lost. Confront the sin, seek forgiveness and answer the call.

Photo by Kevin Carden

DISCUSSION

1) What are your thoughts on Confronting the sin? _____
   _____
   _____
   _____

2) Is there more than one stronghold in which you must confront the
   sin? Yes_____ No_____
   Explain._____
   _____
   _____
   _____

3) What are your thoughts on seeking forgiveness not only from God
   but others as well? _____
   _____
   _____
   _____

4) Are you prepared in the case you are not forgiven by someone you
   may have offended? Yes_____ No_____.
   Do you believe this will effect God's forgiveness of you? Yes __ No __
   If yes, explain: _____
   _____
   _____
   _____

5) What are your plans in Answering the call? _____
   _____
   _____
   _____

6) On this journey called faith, do you believe you will stumble from
   time to time? Yes____ No ____
   How many times does God forgive? _____
   _____
   _____
   _____

7) Does this mean you can go on sinning time after time or are there limits to what God will allow?_____

_____

_____

8) What are your thoughts on the sixty day battle plan? _____

_____

_____

9) Did you find this book helpful in confronting your strongholds?
Yes ____ No ____
Would you recommend this book to a friend?
Yes ____ No____

ABOUT THE AUTHOR

Ernie Stuckey, was born in Brunswick Georgia in 1956. His most important day was on January 8, 2006 when he accepted Jesus Christ as Lord over his life. Ernie excelled in sports in school and has been a successful athletic coach winning three consecutive state championships and a national runner up in softball as well as a 100-game winner in football. Married to his wife, Robyn, for over 40 years, they have two daughters and sons-in-law with four grandchildren. Currently, he serves as an operations manager at the same company for over 30 years with 45 years overall in management.

In 2009, Ernie founded the Family Driven Softball League which creates fellowship among other Christian churches. In 2016, he founded the Christian Men's Association of North Florida. Through regular monthly meetings this organization has promoted men's ministry within local churches. In 2018, Ernie founded Encourage Ministries which provides free spiritual coaching at no cost for those in need. In 2019 Ernie founded Robyn's Hope, a ministry dedicated to help find a cure for Huntington's Disease.

For the past ten years, Ernie has served in several ministry positions including director of men's ministry and director of deacons at a church of more than 1,500 members. He has served as guest speaker for many churches, men's groups and small groups. Ernie has recently returned to where it all started for him at Springhill Baptist church in Fernandina Beach, Florida where he serves as leader of the men's ministry.

ENDNOTES

Cover photo by Kevin Carden (Christianphotoshops.com)
    Sword of the spirit.

Introduction

Photo (Sea oats), by Donna M. Courson

Dedication

Exodus 20:14 King James Version
John 10:10 English Standard version

Chapter One

Stronghold, Merriam-Webster.com
Job 1:12 New International Version
Matthew 8:28-32 English Standard Version
Ed Salvoso quote from www.kenbirks.com/outlines/strongholds
Jeremiah 29:11 New King James Version
Hebrews 12:17 New King James Version
1 Corinthians 10:13 New King James Version
Romans 5:8 New King James Version
John 3:16-17 New Kings Version
2 Corinthians 10:4-6 New King James Version
Discussion on Strongholds

Chapter Two

Bob Barnes, Men Under Construction
Romans 5:3-4 New Living Translation
James 1:3 New International Version
Forbes contributor Dan Diamond
    (Executive Editor for Adviser Boards Dailey
Briefing) Jan. 1, 2013 in forbes.com
Patrick Moreley, *Man in the Mirror*
Wikipedia.org, New Years Resolution
Authentic Manhood *33 The Series*
Hebrews 10:24-25 New King James Version
John 10:10 New King James Version
The Free Dictionary.com, Passing thought
Matthew 5:27-28 New King James Version
Wikipedia.org, Bad Habit
Christian Armor Ministries ChristianArmor.net, Spiritual strongholds
Ephesians 6:11-17 New American Standard version
John 1:5 New International Version
Isaiah 55:11 New King James Version
James 5:16 New International Version
(AA) Alcoholics Anonymous www.neflaa.org/
Jeremiah 16:17 New International Version
Psalm 147:3 New Living Translation
Whisker Rubs by Don Otis
Ephesians 2:8-9 New King James Version
Deuteronomy 31:6 New King James Version
Photo by Kevin Carden (Christianphotoshops.com)
    Man praying over Bible
Discussion on Resolutions

Chapter Three

Psychology today psychology>today.com/basics/addiction
John Kelly PH.D. Contributor to physiology today
    (/blog/whee-science-meets- the-steps)

Matthew 22:35-40 New King James version
John Madden, *Hey wait a minute, I wrote a book*
Revelation 1:3 New King James Version
Romans 12:6-8 New King James Version
Revelation 3:20 New King James Version
Psalm 46:10 New King James Version
1 Kings 10:11-13 New King James Version
Pastor Darryl Bellar, Journey Church, Fernandina Beach Florida
John 10:27 New King James Version
Proverbs 19:8 New Living Translation
Ephesians 5:29 New Living Translation
Deuteronomy 5:9-10 New King James Version
Ezekiel 18:19 New King James Version
Matthew 10:28 New King James Version
Matthew 11:28-30 New King James Version
1 John 2:15-17 New King James Version
Matthew 19:26 New King James Version
Photo by Kevin Carden (Christianphotoshops.com) Cross Bridge
Discussion on Addictions

Chapter Four

Adderall (WebMD)
Exodus 34:7 New King James Version
Proverbs 22:6 New King James Version
Matthew 21:12-13 New King James Version
Mark 3:1-5 New King James Version
Ezekiel 19:19 New King James Version
Galatians 3:13 New King James Version
Romans 12:1-2 New King James Version
Hebrews 12:5-6 New King James Version
Romans 8:28 New International Version
Isaiah 55:8-9 English Standard Version
1 John 4:19 New King James Version
Lamentations 3:21-22 New King James Version
2 Corinthians 12:9-10 New King James Version

2 Peter 3:9 New King James Version
Discussion on Anger

Chapter Five

National Alliance on Mental Illness (NAMI) 2017
Medline Plus medlineplus.gov (National Library of Medicine)
Photo by Donna M. Courson Dock going out to ocean
God will save me...Author unknown
John 16:33 English Standard Version
Matthew 5:4 New King James Version
Philippians 1:21-24 English Standard Version
Charles Swindol Author of Grace Awakening www.goodbread.com
Deuteronomy 31:8 New King James Version
Psalm 34:17 New King James Version
Psalm 40:1-3 New King James Version
1 Peter 5:7 English Standard Version
Romans 8:2 English Standard Version
Romans 8:38-39 English Standard Version
1 Peter 4:12-13 English Standard Version
Isaiah 41:10 English Standard Version
Ezekiel 33:11 New King James Version
Luke 6:37 New King James Version
1 John 3:30 New Living Translation
Psalm 103:12 New Living Translation
John 3:16-17 English Standard Version
Isaiah 43:7 English Standard Version
Genesis 2:7 New King James Version
Genesis 1:31 New King James Version
1 Corinthians 6:19-20 English Standard Version
Ephesians 2:10 English Standard Version
Jeremiah 29:11 English Standard Version
Comment from Billy Graham
Discussion on Depression

www.merriam-webster.com/dictionary/discipline
Timothy 2:22 New King James Version
Proverbs 23:20-21 New King James Version
Hebrews 13:5 New King James Version
Proverbs 6:6-8 New King James Version
Romans 12:19 New King James Version
Galatians 5:26 New King James Version
Jeremiah 9:23-24 New King James Version
Romans 12:16 New International Version
Proverbs 5:23 New Living Translation
Exodus 34:6-7 New King James Version
Romans 10:8-9 New King James Version
Photo by Kevin Carden (Christianphotoshops.com) Erasing sin
2 Timothy 1:7 English Standard Version
Proverbs 10:17 English Standard Version
Proverbs 12:1 English Standard Version
Titus 1:8 English Standard Version
Exodus 20:3 New King James Version
A.W. Tozer www.revival-library.com
Luke 10:27 New King James Version
Ephesians 6:12 New King James Version
Zach Terry (First Baptist Church of Fernandina Beach Florida)
1 Timothy 6:11 New King James Version
1 Corinthians 6:19-20 New King James Version
Sixty day battle plan
Matthew 6:14-15 New King James Version
Proverbs 6:4 New Living Translation
Photo by Kevin Carden (Christianphotoshops.com)
     The Cross and Shadow
Discussion on Discipline

www.activebeat.com (Fear)
Inauguration speech from 1933 by Franklin D. Roosevelt
Photo by Kevin Carden (Christianphotoshops.com) Cast of fear
2 Timothy 1:7 New King James Version
Quote from Rick Warren (christianpost.com)
Quote from John MacArthur (gty.org)
Deuteronomy 30:15 New King James Version
Deuteronomy 30:17-18 New King James Version
1 John 4:18-19 NKJV
Romans 8:38-39 New King James Version
2 Corinthians 10:4-6 New King James Version
2 Peter 1:3 New King James Version
Quote from Max Lacado
Quote from Woodroll Kroll
Quote from Henry Ford
Quote from Pastor Darryl Bellar, Journey Church
Matthew 6:25-27 New King James Version
Philippians 4:6-7 New King James Version
Genesis 3:7-10 New King James Version
Deuteronomy 31:6 New King James Version
Luke 22:41-44 New King James Version
Matthew 27:45-46 New King James Version
Atheists in foxholes (author unknown)
Hebrews 4:14-16 New King James Version
2 Peter 3:9 New King James Version
John 10:10 King James Version
1 Peter 5:7 New International Version
Matthew 6:7-8 New International Version
Romans 8:28 New International Version
Photo of Robyn Stuckey on her flight to California by Ernie Stuckey
Discussion on Fear

Chapter Eight

Definition of Jealousy by Merriam-Webster.com
Definition of Jealousy by Dictionary.com
Bible.org (Two types of jealousy)
Exodus 34:14 New King James Version
Proverbs 14:30 New King James Version
Romans 12:21 New King James Version
Proverbs 27:4 New King James Version
Matthew 18:15-16 New King James Version
2 Timothy 2:22 English Standard Version
1 Timothy 6:11-12 English Standard Version
Psalm 37:4 New King James Version
Four times God says "I will never leave you"
    Deuteronomy 31:8, Hebrews 13:5, Joshua 1:5, 1 Chronicles 28:2
    (All English Standard Version).
Colossians 3:13 English Standard Version
James 5:16 English Standard Version
1 John 1:9 English Standard Version
Hebrews 6:6 New King James Version
Discussion on Jealousy

Chapter Nine

Teacher survey by Van Power
Statistics on a fatherless home by www.fatherhood.com
US Census Bureau (fatherless homes)
fatherlessgeneration.wordpress.com/statistics/
Quote from Mother Teresa
1 Corinthians 13:4-7 New King James Version
Genesis 3:6 New King James Version
Jonah 3:10 New International Version
2 Chronicles 7:14 King James Version
Gone with the wind Producer David O.Selznick
Average Facebook user by www.bigthink.com
Cats in the Cradle by Harry Chapin

Jesus the Carpenter by Faithwork & Economics www.tifwe.org
Mark 6:2-3 New King James Version
Revelation 19:11-16 New King James Version
Hebrews 4:12 New International Version
1 Peter 5:8-11 New King James Version
33 The Series by Authentic manhood
From This Day Forward by Craig Groeschel www.lifechurch.org
False Love by Brad Hambrick Summit Church
Baptist Press www.bpnews.net
Family Driven Faith by Voddie Baucham
Mark 9:35 New International Version
Ephesians 5:25-26 New King James Version
Ephesians 5:22-24 New King James Version
Love & Respect by Dr. Emerson Eggerichs
2 Corinthians 6:14 New International Version
1 Peter 3:1 English Standard Version
Ecclesiastes 4:9-12 New King James Version
Quote from Chuck Lynch
Photo by Kevin Carden (Christianphotoshops.com)
    Family walks to cross
The American Psychological Association Marriage & Divorce
Hebrews 8:12 New King James Version
Psalm 103:12 New King James Version
Discussion on Leading your family

Chapter Ten

John 14:27 New International Version
John 10:10 New International Version
Romans 8:39 New Living Translation
1 John 4:19 New International Version
2 Corinthians 4:17 New Living Translation
Adrian Rogers "Don't worry"
Isaiah 55:8-9 New King James Version
Proverbs 3:5-6 New King James Version
1 Corinthians 3:6 King James Version
Dwayne Sumner on Forgiveness

Matthew 6:14-15 New International Version
Photo by Kevin Carden (Christianphotoshops.com) Bible with nails
Discussion on Forgiveness

Chapter Eleven

Businessweek.com May 4th 2012
U.S. News and World Report
FBI.com
Matthew 7:1-2 New King James Version
Matthew 7:4 New King James Version
Matthew 7:6 New King James Version
Quote from Billy Graham
1 Timothy 1:15 New Living Translation
Ephesians 1:7 English Standard Version
Song of Solomon 7:6-10 English Standard Version
Genesis 3:1-5 New King James Version
1 Peter 3:7 New King James Version
Ben Hall and the Locker Room
Every Mans Battle by Fred Stoeker and Steve Arterburn
1 Corinthians 7:8-9 New International Version
Love and Respect by Dr. Emerson Eggerichs
1 Corinthians 7:2-5 New International Version
Leviticus 18:22 New King James Version
Photo by Kevin Carden (Christianphotoshops.com)
    Man chained to computer
Discussion on Lust

Chapter Twelve

Proverbs 16:18 New King James Version
Deuteronomy 4:2 New American Standard Version
Isaiah 13:11 New King James Version
Isaiah 5:20 New King James Version
Proverbs 4:24 New International Version
Proverbs 8:13 New International Version
Definition of Pride

Proverbs 11:2 English Standard Version
Luke 14:11 English Standard Version
John 13:1-7 New International Version
Mark 9:35 New International Version
Photo by Kevin Carden (Christianphotoshops.com) Narrow way
Matthew 11:28-30 New International Version
Discussion on Pride

Chapter Thirteen

Atmosphere by Scott Krippayne, Andy Chrisman & Jamie Kenny
Three-legged stool by Jackie Hayes
When you want to hear from God by Adriana Dunton
Matthew 7:15 New International Version
1 Peter 5:8 New International Version
1 Corinthians 10:13 New International Version
Photo by Kevin Carden (Christianphotoshops.com) Powerful Bible
Ephesians 5:25 New International Version
1 Corinthians 2:1-5 World English Bible
Discussion on Maintaining success
Picture of Ernie Stuckey by Robyn Stuckey

About the Author

Back cover Hebrews 6:19 New King James Version
Back cover photo by Kevin Carden (Christianphotoshop.com)
    Anchor reaching up

Printed in the United States
By Bookmasters